THE HUMANITY
AND DIVINITY OF
CHRIST

THE HUMANITY
AND DIVINITY OF
CHRIST

A STUDY OF PATTERN
IN CHRISTOLOGY

BY

JOHN KNOX

Professor Emeritus, Union Theological Seminary
Professor of New Testament,
Episcopal Theological Seminary of the Southwest

CAMBRIDGE
AT THE UNIVERSITY PRESS
1967

Published by the Syndics of the Cambridge University Press
Bentley House, 200 Euston Road, London, N.W. 1
American Branch: 32 East 57th Street, New York, N.Y. 10022

© Cambridge University Press 1967

Library of Congress Catalogue Card Number: 67-10349

Printed in the United States of America

CONTENTS

Dedicated, in love and hope, to two god-children, Peter Anders Edman and John Samuel Robinson, and to John Smith Prather Beeland, whom I baptized, and to their parents, with the prayer that all of us may continue Christ's faithful soldiers and servants unto our life's end

INTRODUCTION

My purpose in this essay is limited and comparatively simple: I wish to lift up for consideration the several ways in which the early Church dealt with what has always been the central problem of christology, namely, the humanity of Christ, the divine Lord, and in this way help, if I may, to clarify our own thoughts about him. By 'the humanity of Christ' I mean, quite plainly, the fact or apparent fact that Jesus was a man.

The propriety of such an undertaking may be challenged, and perhaps a few words of justification are appropriate. Someone may ask: 'Is what you have just said true of the primitive christology? Was the early Christian concerned with the issue of the humanity (or divinity) of Jesus? Have you not brought to the New Testament an essentially modern problem? And are you not, therefore, in danger of distorting what its writers were meaning to say by forcing them to answer a question they did not confront or consider?' This critical reaction is not merely hypothetical. An actual reader of the opening chapters of this book has said to me: 'I have the feeling that 'humanity–divinity' is not the right exegetical frame of reference. This is not wholly with the grain of the documents.'

I see the truth and feel the force of this objection; and yet I do not regard it as fatal. It is true that the words 'humanity' and 'divinity' (or 'human' and 'divine') hardly appear in the New Testament, and never in a christological connection. But too much can easily be made of the presence or absence of particular words. The realities to which, for us at least, these words answer were undoubtedly present from the beginning—namely, the man Jesus most surely remembered and the heavenly Lord most surely known—and the age-old problem of christology is implicit in that fact. For how could he be both? And since there was never any lack of certainty and clarity about his present exaltation, the question was bound to be concerned mostly with his nature and career as a man. It can be argued that among the New Testament writers—certainly among all but the very latest of them—this question was not consciously asked or answered. But this does not mean that the more significant writers did not have their own characteristic ways of thinking about the nature and meaning of the human life of Jesus, and that these ways were not in part determined, whether they knew it or not, by their belief in his divine Lordship. In a word, the later preoccupation of the Church with the problem of how Jesus could be both God and man was not a development new and alien, but represented a continuation of a process of reflection which began surely as early as Paul's time, however strange the terms of later discussions would have seemed to him, or even the existence of the discussions themselves.

We are concerned in these chapters entirely with the Church's thought, and not at all with the problem of Jesus' own understanding of his nature and role.[1] Such ideas as I may have on the latter theme are presented in my book *The Death of Christ*, and I am intending neither to alter nor to develop further what is set forth there. As

[1] Several chapters of this book were presented at the Bangor Theological Seminary as the Francis B. Denio Lectures and the first of them in a somewhat different form was published in the *Alumni Bulletin* of that institution. I am grateful to the editor of the *Bulletin* for permission to make some use of that lecture in this publication, as well as to the President, the faculty, and others at Bangor for many courtesies at the time of my visit.

a matter of fact, christology in the distinctively Christian sense must, almost by definition, be thought of as a post-resurrection development, an aspect of the Church's thought about how, and through whom, it came to be. In any case, we shall be concerned with it only as such.

The book falls into two nearly equal parts. The first three chapters will be primarily historical and if they stood alone might, for all their brevity, presume to some such title as 'Christology in the New Testament'. The same descriptive phrase (as distinguished from, say, 'The Christology of the New Testament') might perhaps be applied to other books of mine which also deal with this same general theme but make no attempt, either separately or together, to do so in a systematic or exhaustive way.[1] The qualification indicated in this last clause will obviously apply, with special aptness, to the present brief book. We shall not be examining one by one the titles of Jesus (as Taylor, Cullmann, and Hahn have done)[2] or any particular title (with Otto, Duncan, Bowman, Manson, both W. and T. W., Hooker, Zimmerli and Jeremias, Tödt,[3] and many others); nor shall I be

[1] I have in mind here particularly *The Man Christ Jesus* (1941), *Christ the Lord* (1945), *On the Meaning of Christ* (1947), the three being now published together as *Jesus : Lord and Christ* (New York: Harper and Row, 1958); *The Death of Christ* (New York and Nashville: Abingdon Press, 1958), already cited; and *The Church and the Reality of Christ* (New York: Harper and Row, 1962). I presume to mention these books because the present work so constantly presupposes them.

[2] V. Taylor, *The Names of Jesus* (London: Macmillan, 1953); O. Cullmann, *The Christology of the New Testament* (Philadelphia: Westminster Press, 1959); F. Hahn, *Christologische Hoheitstitel* (Göttingen: Vanderhoeck and Rupprecht, 1963).

[3] R. Otto, *The Kingdom of God and the Son of Man* (London and Grand Rapids: Zondervan, 1938–9); G. Duncan, *Jesus, Son of Man* (New York: Macmillan, 1949); J. W. Bowman, *The Intention of Jesus* (Philadelphia: Westminster Press, 1943); W. Manson, *Jesus the Messiah* (Philadelphia: Westminster Press, 1946); T. W. Manson, *The Servant-Messiah* (Cambridge University Press, 1953); M. D. Hooker, *Jesus and the Servant* (London: S.P.C.K., 1959); W. Zimmerli and J. Jeremias,

attempting anything like a systematic treatment of the several writers of the New Testament in their chronological order (in the manner of Rawlinson)[1] or of the christology of any single writer (as MacNeill[2] has done for Hebrews and Brückner, Andrews,[3] and others have done for Paul). My purpose is both more simple and more general. I wish to suggest and defend a way of understanding the *structure* of the New Testament christology as a whole, a way of seeing the *pattern* of its development. And we shall seek this understanding, as I have said, by following as a kind of clue the changing ways in which Jesus' humanity was interpreted and emphasized.

The latter half of the book will be concerned primarily with the problem of how the modern Christian is to think of the human Christ, and with the continuing meaning and relevance of this same structure or pattern. Here the limits of my purpose and the absence of any pretentions to comprehensiveness and adequacy will be, I hope, even more apparent. In both sections of this discussion I shall be trying to indicate a path through a large and complicated field, not to survey the field as a whole, much less to explore its several parts. But to say this is not to disparage the importance of the undertaking. Is not a viable path what we most need? Knowing the facts is useless unless one also sees how to walk among them.

The Servant of God (London: S.C.M., 1965); H. E. Tödt, *The Son of Man in the Synoptic Tradition* (London: S.C.M. Press, 1965).

[1] A. E. J. Rawlinson, *The New Testament Doctrine of Christ* (London: Longmans, Green, 1926). The important work of R. H. Fuller, *The Foundations of New Testament Christology* (New York: Charles Scribner's Sons, 1965), does not neatly fit any of the categories I am now using, but it calls for mention.

[2] H. L. MacNeill, *The Christology of the Epistle to the Hebrews* (Chicago: University of Chicago Press, 1914).

[3] M. Brückner, *Die Entstehung der paulinischen Christologie* (Strassburg, 1903); E. Andrews, *The Meaning of Christ for Paul* (Nashville: Abingdon Press, 1949).

I

THREE ANCIENT CHRISTOLOGIES

The question to be considered in these opening chapters can be simply asked: what was the role of the human Jesus in the New Testament story of God's act in Christ? But, like most questions about ideas in history, it cannot be so simply answered. The story of the Christ appears in the New Testament in several forms—or perhaps it would be more accurate to say that several stages in the development of the story are found there—so that the significance of Jesus' human life is not always grasped or set forth in the same way. There are differences among the New Testament writers both as regards the purpose and function of the humanity and as regards its character and reality. One of the theses which will appear in this discussion is that there is a correlation between these two—that is, between the way a New Testament author conceived of the role or purpose of the humanity (the reasons for it) and the realism with which he thought of it; between the answers he would have given to the question 'Why did there have to be a human Christ?' and the question 'How human —that is, how fully or normally human—was he?'[1] We do not need to suppose that these questions were actually asked in order to see how they would have been answered. Nor does it follow from the fact that the questions were not explicitly raised that these implicit answers were not important. We are not proposing, then, an irrelevant

[1] O. R. Buckwalter, 'Nature and Significance of the Humanity of Jesus in the New Testament' (unpublished Ph.D. dissertation, Columbia University, 1953).

issue when we inquire: what was the place of Jesus'
humanity in the primitive Christian mythology?

The use of the phrase 'primitive Christian mythology'
may serve to remind us of a distinction to be discussed
more fully later but deserving some attention at the outset—the distinction between the significance of the
humanity in the story or myth of the Christ and its
meaning in the actual existence of the early Church.
Now this distinction between myth and existence, while
of the greatest importance, is not the most easy to make,
not to say maintain, with any consistency. Speaking
generally, we may say that a myth of the kind we find in
the New Testament comes into being within a religious
community to express the realized concrete meaning of
the community's existence. It therefore stands in the
closest possible—probably in a quite inseparable—
relation to that concrete meaning; but it is not to be
simply identified with it. The story is a representation;
it is not the thing itself. It is an image or a series of
images; it is not the reality to which the images point or
for which they stand.

In the case we are examining, the concrete reality is
the actual inner existence of the Church; and in that
existence the human Jesus has an inalienable and very
secure place: he is *remembered* there. This memory of a
man, a particular man, is absolutely essential to the
Church's being. So also, of course, is its knowledge of
him as living and present—that is, as being no longer
among the dead, as being its Lord. Indeed, the distinctive character of the Church's existence among other
human communities consists in the fact that it thus remembers and thus knows. This is the concrete, experienced meaning of both the resurrection and the Spirit.

The phrase 'Jesus Christ our Lord' designates, not primarily an historical individual in the past, nor yet a character in a symbolic story, but a present reality actually experienced within the common life. The story arose to account, as well as might be, for so marvellous a fact of experience and to set forth and convey, as adequately as possible, its realized inner meaning and effect. It is obviously the consequence, not the source, of what the Church most truly knows—and the remembered Jesus, as well as his continuing reality, belongs to this most basic and certain knowledge.

But if it is important for us to recognize that the Church's memory of Jesus and its experience of his living Presence belong essentially to its existence and not to any process of what has come to be called 'mytho-logizing', it is almost equally important that we see quite clearly that when, in the earliest period, the first step was taken toward expressing or communicating the concrete content, the realized inner meaning, of this existence, not to speak of trying to account for it, or ex-plain it, a process of mythologizing had begun. This is true because this meaning was realized as a *divine* mean-ing, and one cannot express such meaning, or even clearly realize it for oneself, without resort to mytho-logical speech. We find ourselves saying, 'In the fullness of time God came to us in the person of his Son to redeem us from our enemies', or speaking in some other such way; and immediately we are telling a story, making a picture, dramatizing, mythologizing. Actually, we cannot avoid such imaginative terms, no matter how factually or plainly we try to speak. The Christian gospel, at its simplest, is an announcement of something God has done for us men and our salvation. It is not unlikely that when we use the word 'done' in this connection, we have already begun to speak mythologically;[1] but whether that can be said or not, certainly we cannot proceed to describe, even in the simplest terms, *what* God has done in Christ, or to explain *why* he has done it, or just *how* this action has accomplished his purpose—we cannot begin to speak, or even to think, of such matters without using mythological terms.

We may not always recognize this character of our speech, and for many purposes it is quite as well that we do not. Since we cannot express the distinctive concrete reality of the Christian existence except in terms of a story of what God did in Christ, reality and story flow together and the one partakes of the other. But for purposes of discussion the two can be distinguished, and it is with the story that we shall be most concerned. More particularly, we shall be asking the question: How did the humanity of Jesus 'figure' in it? What setting or settings for it, and therefore what explanation or explanations of it, did the developing mythology provide in the New Testament period?

Because Paul and the writer to the Hebrews have a central place in this development, they will make the largest claims on our attention. But we shall be making constant reference backward to the more primitive preaching, as it may be recovered from the Synoptic

[1] An important part of the current discussion, chiefly among German scholars, about the 'demythologizing' which Bultmann has insisted needs to be done—and done in a certain way—has been concerned with this question. Much depends obviously on how the words 'myth' and 'mythological' are defined. Bultmann holds that we can speak of God's *action* in Christ without being mythological; some of his critics have a different view. For our purposes the point is not significant; but for a report of the very important discussion as a whole, including the original essay by Bultmann and further contributions by him and others, see H. W. Bartsch, *Kerygma und Mythos* (in several volumes from 1948 onwards), translated by R. H. Fuller, *Kerygma and Myth* (London: S.P.C.K.), also in several volumes, the first of which appeared in 1953.

Gospels and Acts, and forward to the later and theologically more developed thought of the Fourth Gospel. Observation of the several points thus roughly marked will enable us, I believe, to chart the general course of the primitive Christian effort to realize, and to represent, the nature and meaning of the human life of Christ.

If we recognize that the Christian Church as a distinctive historical community actually had its beginning in the association of some men and women with Jesus, the teacher and prophet from Nazareth in Galilee, we shall not expect to find that his humanity constituted any problem for the earliest Church or was at first invested with any special theological significance. He would have been thought of simply as the human being he was. It would not have occurred to anyone to affirm that Jesus was human, for the obvious reason that it would not have occurred to anyone that he might have been anything else. And one would no more have asked 'Why was Jesus human?' than one would ever ask the same question about oneself or another. To be sure, he had been an extraordinary man, 'mighty in word and deed'— had not events proved that he was to be the Anointed of God, the promised Messiah of Israel and the nations?— nevertheless, the question 'Could he have been really a man at all?' would have been excluded. The experience of life with him would have been too recent and the remembrance of him too vivid and uncomplicated to allow for even the asking of such a question. All of this being true, then, we should not have expected the earliest theological reflection of the Church to be concerned either with the fact of Jesus' humanity or with the reasons for it. That fact would simply have been taken

5

for granted as obvious and indisputable, and as calling for neither emphasis nor explanation.

This expectation of what the first form of the story would have been in this respect is fully confirmed by such documentary indications as we have of the most primitive preaching. A critical reading of the first few chapters of Acts confirms the conclusion which even a casual reading suggests: the original gospel was that Jesus, 'the holy and righteous one', 'crucified and killed by lawless men', God had raised up from among the dead and had exalted to a place of lordship at his own 'right hand'. From this place the Spirit had already been sent and from it Christ himself would soon come to exercise the messianic functions which God had entrusted to him—that is, to judge the present world and to inaugurate the New Age.

In such a story[1] the simple actuality of the humanity

---

[1] We face in this discussion a semantic problem of great difficulty. In speaking of the Church's dramatic representation of the meaning of Christ, shall we use the word 'myth', or 'story', or some other term? The word 'myth' has so pejorative a meaning for many Christians that they shrink from its use in such a connection. It is also true that 'myth' may be thought of in such close connection with nature and its cycles as to seem inapplicable to a story which is centrally concerned with an historical happening. In some earlier lectures I sought to demonstrate the propriety of the term in speaking of the Church's christology in its more fully developed forms, and in so far as I use it in this discussion I am doing so in the sense I sought to define there (*Myth and Truth* [Charlottesville, Va.: University Press of Virginia, 1964]). In the present work, however, I shall speak very frequently of 'story', meaning the content of the gospel as such, whether mythological or not, and in whatever degree. In that most primitive adoptionist christology, for example, which we are now considering, the human life of Jesus is obviously a part of the 'story' but it is not so clear that we could speak of it as a part of any 'myth'. In that 'story', the mythological element seems to enter only after the human career has ended. The broad term 'story' may be employed to cover the whole range of christological development in a way the word 'myth' fails to do. Another reason for my preferring in some connections the terms 'story' and 'drama' is that I find a literary analogy often appropriate and illuminating (note the use I shall later make of 'prologue').

was in no sense or degree compromised. Not only could it be whole and intact, but it was also subject to no theological or mythological pressure of any kind. The distinctively divine, the theologically significant, action began with the resurrection, and the humanity of Jesus could be for the Church's *thought* as 'natural' and un-complicated as there is every reason to believe it was in its memory.

I have said that the prevalence in the most primitive period of such a christology as this—it is sometimes called 'adoptionism'—is clearly indicated in the opening part of Acts, especially in some of the speeches of Peter and others. Not everyone agrees that this is true;[1] and even in as untechnical a discussion as this one wants to be, some attention must be paid to the objectors. These have no trouble showing that the author of Luke-Acts had a higher or more advanced, a less simple, christology than the adoptionism I have described. The whole treat-ment of the earthly life of Jesus in the Gospel section of his work and many an allusion to it in the Acts sec-tion indicate beyond question that he did not think of Jesus' messiahship as having been conferred on him only after his human career had ended. Jesus was always 'Son of God'; he was not adopted or installed as such, whether at the resurrection or earlier—or, for that matter, later.

The question, however, is not whether the author of Luke-Acts held an adoptionist christology, but whether evidence for the primitive existence of such a christology is to be found in his work. I do not see how we can escape the conclusion that it is. To cite the clearest example, Acts 2:36 ('God has made this Jesus, whom you

[1] For example, a very recent study, S. S. Smalley, 'The Christology of Acts', *The Expository Times*, LXXIII (1962), 358 ff.

crucified, both Lord and Messiah' [N.E.B.[1]])—how can this passage be interpreted to mean anything else than that the man Jesus, crucified simply as such, was at the resurrection exalted to his present messianic status? Once we acknowledge the presence in Luke-Acts of earlier source materials, claimed and adapted by its author, but (whether through intentional restraint or through oversight or lack of care) only partially assimilated to his own theological position and outlook, we shall not be troubled by finding other passages in which a different christology, belonging presumably to a later stage in the development of the Church's thought, is clearly defined.[2]

We conclude, then, that the earliest christology was adoptionist. We should have expected it to be, and there are unmistakable signs that it was. I repeat that in such a way of picturing and explaining the reality of Christ, his humanity constitutes no problem and is a matter of no special theological interest. It is assumed as the obvious background for God's action in raising Jesus from

[1] Quotations from the New Testament are from either the Revised Standard Version or from the New English Bible (N.E.B.). Quotations from the latter are designated as such in the text.

[2] John A. T. Robinson believes he can find an even earlier stratum in Acts than that represented by 2:36. He holds that 'in the most primitive christology of all' Jesus did not become the Christ even at his resurrection, but *would become* the Christ when the time came for him to return and to function as such in the final Judgement. I do not find the evidence for this earlier phase convincing and see no adequate reason for doubting that for the first believers the resurrection was also the moment of Jesus' exaltation to messiahship and Lordship. But the point I am making—namely, that the earliest christology was adoptionist—is not affected by Bishop Robinson's thesis. See his article in the *Journal of Theological Studies*, N.S., VII (1956), 177 ff., reprinted in *Twelve New Testament Studies* (London: S.C.M. Press, 1962), pp. 139 ff. Cf. R. Bultmann, *Theology of the New Testament* (New York: Charles Scribner's Sons, 1951), I, 33 ff. A fuller discussion of Bishop Robinson's position in the indicated article may be found in my essay, 'The "Prophet" in New Testament Christology', in Richard Norris (ed.), *Lux in Lumine: Essays to Honor W. Norman Pittenger* (New York: Seabury Press, 1966).

the dead and investing him with messiahship. It is the first act in a drama of which only the second is divinely significant.

But this form of the story could hardly have become the final one. Although it corresponded closely with the actual experience of the earliest community of Jesus' disciples, who remembered Jesus in the flesh and now, in the Spirit, knew him as Christ the Lord, it did not accord with the growing sense of the importance and the divine significance of the earthly career. That career, it was now realized, had meanings which at the time were hidden, whether because of man's blindness or because it belonged to the inscrutable purpose of God to conceal them. The story, to be true and adequate, must be altered so as to comprehend and express this deep and mysterious significance. One might have expected the effort at adaptation, no less real for being undeliberate or even unconscious, to take the form of a rewriting of the first act of the two-act drama, the act dealing with the human career, with a view to bringing out its hidden deeper meaning. Such a rewriting eventually occurred, as we shall see. But, in the first instance, the more adequate effect was sought, not through the revision of the 'play' as it had been written, but through the addition of a 'prologue'. Back of the human career lay a divine pre-existence.

In a sense this affirmation of pre-existence was implicit in the story from the beginning. Even in the preaching in early Acts the death of Jesus was 'according to the definite plan and foreknowledge of God'. Actually, it would have been quite impossible for any primitive Jewish Christian to entertain even for a little while the notion that God had merely happened to find a man

9

worthy of becoming the Messiah. It would have followed ineluctably upon the primitive Church's acknowledgement of Jesus as the Christ that God should have known him as such before the foundation of the world. But there is obviously only a short step from the idea of this kind of pre-existence in the mind of God to the conception of a pre-existing hypostasis, a pre-existent being more personal and objective. J. A. T. Robinson speaks of Jesus' pre-existence '...as the equivalent in Greek terms of his "foreordination"'.[1] This seems to suggest that the idea of pre-existence did not emerge till the Church had left its originally Jewish milieu. This may or may not be true (and may or may not be Bishop Robinson's meaning). But there can be no doubt about the close connection, the virtual equivalence, of the two ideas. The affirmation of Jesus' pre-existence was all but implicit in the affirmation of God's foreknowledge of him and was bound to have become explicit eventually, whether in a Jewish or a Greek environment.[2]

I have presented elsewhere the reasons for assurance that this happened very soon.[3] Paul not only speaks of the pre-existence of Christ but obviously takes for

---

[1] *Twelve New Testament Studies*, p. 143.

[2] It would surely be a mistake to decide that the conception of Jesus' personal pre-existence could not have had currency in a Palestinian Jewish environment. To know this, we have only to recall the prevalence, in certain circles at least, of the idea of the Son of Man, a divine being. If Jesus was identified with this being, as he seems to be in the earliest gospel traditions, pre-existence, in some sense, was being ascribed to him. The phrase 'in some sense' is important here. A great variety in the meaning of pre-existence is possible. For example, R. Otto (*The Kingdom of God and the Son of Man*) interprets Jesus' own consciousness of identity with the heavenly Son of Man somewhat in terms of a prevalent Oriental way of thinking according to which every man has a heavenly counterpart. Jesus was aware of himself as being implicitly or proleptically the Son of Man, an identity into which he would later fully enter.

[3] *Jesus, Lord and Christ* (New York: Harper and Row, 1958), pp. 150 f. Cf. Rom. 15:3; II Cor. 8:9; Phil. 2:5 ff.

granted that the conception was a familiar one to his readers and that they did not need to be convinced of its truth. He never explains it or argues for it. He never makes a point of it. This means that, among his own churches at least, and presumably elsewhere, the idea was well established when his major letters were written, within fifteen or twenty years of Jesus' crucifixion. There are good reasons for believing that the Church's attribution of a divine pre-existence to Jesus was not, as it has sometimes been thought to be, the final step in a gradual process of pressing back the moment of his 'adoption' to an earlier and earlier time—from resurrection, to transfiguration, to baptism, to birth—until finally it was pushed out of the earthly life entirely and the idea of pre-existence was demanded. Such a process would have required time and could hardly have been completed early enough to account for the general acceptance of the idea in the period of Paul's letters. Rather, we are given grounds for believing—what would also seem inherently probable—that reflection on the resurrection and on the post-resurrection status of Christ led directly and immediately to the affirmation of his pre-existence.[1] One may be fairly sure, then, that this affirmation belonged to the original form of the Hellenistic Christian confession, if indeed it had not already become a part of the primitive Palestinian preaching. But whatever may be concluded on this point, it is clear that we are now dealing with a fresh phase or period in the development of the story; and our question is: what happened to the human career of Jesus in this form of it?

The answer, I think, is: at the outset, nothing at all.

[1] *Ibid*. pp. 145 ff. I am cheered by Bishop Robinson's agreement with this way of placing the pre-existence in the primitive christological development (*Twelve N.T. Studies*, p. 143).

The conception of the humanity of Jesus remained exactly as in the earlier form. A prologue had been added to the story, but the story itself was unchanged. The assertion of pre-existence was at first an assertion only about the context or background of Jesus' human exist-ence, not about its nature or intrinsic character. In its inner quality it was still the normal human existence it had been in the more primitive story and was indeed remembered as having been in fact. If the word 'adop-tion' can be used as a label for the earlier phase (a man made at the resurrection Lord and Christ), the term 'kenosis' (emptying) can be employed as a convenient tag for what I am seeking to define as the second phase in this development. A pre-existing divine being 'emptied' himself and became a man—precisely that man who because he was 'obedient to death, even the death of the cross', was 'highly exalted' and given the name of Lord.[1]

A question may properly be raised as to whether such a form of the story ever existed. In reply, it must be con-ceded that nowhere in the New Testament is just this story consistently told; and proof of its ever having been extant is quite impossible. As we have seen, however, the same thing can be said about the first stage, the primitive adoptionism. Just because that stage so quickly passed, one must find indications of its one-time exist-

[1] Phil. 2:5-11. It is, of course, from this passage that the term 'kenosis' is derived. The use of that term and related words like kenotic and kenoticism in speaking of this *story* is to be distinguished sharply from the use of the same words to designate the modern theological position associated with the names of Charles Gore, H. R. Mackintosh and others. Some discussion of this position will be found in Chapter 6. Both of these usages must be distinguished from the use of the term being made in the current decade by T. J. J. Altizer and a few others. For a bibliography of this strange, partly relevant, but surely transitory 'theology', known by the label 'death of God', see J. A. Sanders, in the *Union Seminary Quarterly Review*, XXI (1966), 182-4.

ence in deeper strata in the tradition than any of the New Testament books in its final form represents. So, likewise, we must say that the second phase in the story's growth was also very brief and in its purity and simplicity had ceased to exist when even the earliest New Testament writing was composed. One must look for evidences of it in the traces it has left in later writings. These appear, as I believe we shall see, especially in Paul and the Epistle to the Hebrews, but are not altogether absent from the Synoptic Gospels and other New Testament books.

As in the case of the earlier adoptionism, however, one does not need to rely only on this evidence; there is an *a priori* consideration of great importance. If it is true that in the original (the adoptionist) form of the story a man, whose full and normal manhood was simply assumed or taken for granted, was made Lord and Christ, and if it is also true that the assertion of the pre-existence of this man, inferred directly and immediately from the fact of his present exaltation, was simply added to this story as a kind of prologue, then it follows that there must have been a stage, however brief, in the story's evolution when the pre-existence and the normal human career were both *there*, juxtaposed in the sharpest contrast, and the idea of kenosis was fully present. If the two premises are accepted as true, I do not see how the conclusion can be avoided. We are forced, then, to regard kenosis as a distinct second phase in the development of the Church's christology.

Each of the two phases we have so far considered had, as we have seen, only a very brief existence; and since they antedated all of our New Testament books, neither has left a clear and consistent exemplar among our literary sources. The phase to which we now turn is quite different in both respects. Not only do all of the New Testament writings, in so far as they exhibit any christological pattern, exemplify this next stage in the development we are considering—we may call it 'incarnationism'—but it must also be said that for what proved to be orthodox Christianity this stage has been the indefinitely continuing one.

Still another difference can be cited. Both the primitive adoptionism and the later kenoticism were relatively simple pictures: in the first case, a man is exalted to be Lord and Christ; and, in the second, a divine being empties himself of his divine nature and status and becomes a man, who then in virtue of some characteristic or achievement of his human career is exalted, just as in the earlier story, to the same high office. So simple is each story that it can be thought of as coming suddenly and full-blown into existence. The moment those who remembered Jesus recognized him as their risen Lord, the first story had taken its essential shape; and the moment he was pictured as having been pre-existent in heaven, the second story was fully in being. Each story is simple and definite in its essential structure, and it is difficult to conceive of any wide variation within either. But this is not true of what we are calling (for lack of a more specific term) incarnationism. It is less clear-cut in its structure and more diversified in its actual forms. For this reason it cannot be described as a new story. It is an interim between stories—a stage in the basic story's development.

This stage can perhaps be best described as that in which what I have called the first act in the original two-act drama was being adjusted to conform to what has been termed the prologue. Ordinarily, the prologue of a literary work—particularly, a novel or play—does not exert any pressure upon the plot of the story the author is telling, for the reason that it was created precisely in order to fit the plot, to provide an anticipatory explanation of it, to make it more intelligible, or credible, or significant. The story, we may suppose in such a case, will already have been fully written, the action of the drama will have been fully plotted; but now the author realizes that the reader or viewer will be helped to grasp the full meaning of the action if he is told of something which happened far away or long ago, something connected very remotely, if at all, with the characters or plot of the novel or play itself. A prologue, therefore, seems indicated. Ideally, the prologue, while entirely consonant with the action of the story and providing an appropriate background for the understanding of it, lies quite outside the story proper. The adding of the prologue does not require changes in the original narrative. Far from raising problems, its whole intention and effect will be to forestall problems which the story might otherwise leave in the reader's mind.

When we turn from this literary form to what we have called the prologue to the Church's story of the Christ, we can see that the analogy up to a point holds true. The assertion of Jesus' pre-existence provided what seemed the necessary background for his having been raised from the dead and made Lord and Christ. It helped to make more intelligible and acceptable, especially for a Greek Christian perhaps, this mighty 'second act' in the original drama. But here the analogy breaks down, for this prologue did not merely anticipate and deal with difficulties in the story as it stood (as a proper prologue should), but it also created new difficulties. The questions it raised for what I have called the first act were as serious as those it answered for the second.

For how, one was bound to ask, could a heavenly Person, especially when (as soon happened) he was all but identified with God himself, actually have become the authentic human being Jesus was remembered, and theretofore had been represented, as being? Could such a One have ever become a true man? Given even a little reflection on the pre-existence, this question was inevitable, and the history of the Church's struggle with the christological question from a time at least as early as Paul till the present moment has been the history of its attempts to integrate the apparent implications of the pre-existence into the original and basic story of the man Jesus, remembered in life and death, and now exalted to be God's Anointed and our Lord. The prologue, in other words, insisted on becoming the first act in the drama, and the original first act, now become the second, had consequently to be rewritten.

This 'rewriting' was complete only in docetism, the third and final story, with its forthright denial that Christ was ever a true man at all. He *seemed* to be—and it was important for our salvation that he should have *appeared* as such—but actually he was not. He was actually the divine being he had always been and, in the nature of the case, could not have ceased to be. His humanity was a disguise he wore for a while or, better perhaps, a role he played. This third story resembles the other two in its logical coherency, its definiteness, and its simplicity. Like them also, it is not consistently represented in the canon, standing just beyond the limits of orthodoxy on the later side, just as adoptionism and kenoticism do on the earlier. But docetism was at one time widely prevalent, and I do not believe we can understand the orthodox or catholic christology unless we keep it in mind as the logical endpoint of the development to which that christology belongs.

Perhaps some rough diagrams will be useful at this point. If the original adoptionism may be represented thus:

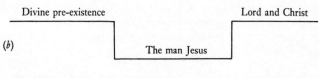

(a) Lord and Christ / The man Jesus

then what I have labelled kenoticism would look like this:

(b) Divine pre-existence / Lord and Christ / The man Jesus

and the final docetism like this:

(c) The eternal Lord / The human appearance

It must be said, however, that although docetism may have been final in the sense of being the logical conclusion of the development we have been seeking to trace, it was not the form of the story which the Church was willing finally to accept. Docetism was rejected, not only for theological reasons we shall later speak of, but also because it constituted an intolerable denial of essential elements in the Church's life, namely, its remembrance of Jesus and its sense of being rooted in history, especially in the history of Israel. Since, however, the earlier forms of the story had also been found inadequate, this rejection of docetism meant that the Church had finally to settle for a christology which might perhaps be described as a 'revised' story, or as falling between stories, or as being a mixture of stories, but which cannot be said to tell a clear, consistent story of its own. Paul, the Synoptic Gospels and Acts, Hebrews, the Fourth Gospel, and, less significantly, the rest of the New Testament writings show us various stages in the development of this christology. To a consideration of this diversified picture, this mixed, or broken, christological pattern, we now turn.

THE
LIMITS OF INCARNATIONISM

We begin with Paul, not only because he is the earliest
Christian writer whose work has survived, but also
because his particular kind of 'incarnationism' comes
nearest to being kenoticism and is thus, indirectly, an
important witness to the latter's having existed. To give
something of a frame to this discussion, I may add that
at the opposite pole within the canonical literature is the
Fourth Gospel, which comes almost as near to docetism
as Paul does to the more primitive views. Thus Paul and
John (whatever the latter's date) set, at least approxi-
mately,[1] the limits of possible divergency within what
we are calling incarnationism, and all the rest of the New
Testament books find their place somewhere between
them.

There are passages in Paul which, taken alone and
without reference to context, would suggest that he
shared in the primitive adoptionism. One thinks, for
example, of a clause near the beginning of Romans
(1:3): '...concerning his Son, who was descended from
David according to the flesh and designated Son of God
in power according to the Spirit of holiness by his
resurrection from the dead.' This statement seems
entirely in harmony with the Acts text (2:36) in which

[1] This qualification is needed because there might be a question
whether the Epistle to the Hebrews does not represent, even better than
Paul, the kenotic boundary of incarnationism. Certainly in this respect,
as we shall see, Paul and Hebrews are very close together. But Paul is the
earlier, and therefore I cite him here.

we have found the primitive adoptionist view most clearly stated: 'God has made him both Lord and Christ, this Jesus whom you crucified.' The same conception is unmistakably present in the background of Phil. 2:8-9, especially when the force of the 'therefore' (διό) is taken into account: 'And being found in human form he humbled himself and became obedient unto death, even death on a cross. Therefore God has highly exalted him and bestowed on him the name which is above every name...'

But if such passages (and many others could be cited), with their emphasis upon the decisive character of what happened to Jesus at the resurrection, seem to reflect the persistence of the early adoptionism, other passages put beyond doubt Paul's belief in Jesus' pre-existence. Often the two ideas—pre-existence and adoption—are found closely associated in the same context. It is not unlikely, for example, that in Rom. 1:3, the phrase 'his Son' implies, and was meant to suggest, pre-existence; and the sentences I have quoted from Philippians as reflecting an adoptionist view belong to the conclusion of a paragraph which begins: 'Though he was in the form of God, he did not count equality with God a thing to be grasped but emptied himself, taking the form of a servant, being born in the likeness of men.' And this is not, by any means, the only place where Paul's assumption of the pre-existence unmistakably appears.

It is much less clear just how he conceived or pictured the pre-existent One. Was he the Son of Man of Jewish apocalyptic, the heavenly being in the form of a man whom, it was expected in certain quarters, God was to send as the promised Saviour? Did Paul think that in Jesus this Son of Man had come to initiate the New Age and that he would return to consummate it? There are those who understand the references to 'the one man Jesus Christ' in Rom. 5:12–21 and to 'the man from heaven' in I Cor. 15:20–2, 45–9 to reflect this kind of apocalyptic imagery. This imagery, as Reitzenstein, Kraeling,[1] and others have pointed out, represents a particular (the Hebrew Jewish) form of a myth widely prevalent in the ancient Near East, the myth of Anthropos, a heavenly Man, primal and archetypal as well as eschatological. It is suggested that this mythological idea, in sublimated form, is present in Philo's distinction between ideal Man, whose creation he finds in the first chapter of Genesis, and the actual man (and woman) whose separate and later creation is recounted in the second chapter of that book.[2] Did Paul think of Jesus as being in his pre-existence this ideal heavenly Man? I should find it more plausible to believe that he did if he had ever used the phrase Son of Man or in any other way had made explicit reference to this way of understanding the pre-existent Christ. Actually, he seems to be rejecting it when he points out with some emphasis (I Cor. 15:46) that Christ as saving Man is the *second* man. *As man* Christ is always represented as *following* Adam and never as preceding him. Still, one cannot rule out the possibility that Paul, at least sometimes, thought of Christ's pre-existence in terms borrowed from this kind of theological speculation.

More can be said for the view that he conceived of the pre-existent One, in terms derived from Hellenistic Jewish and Greek religious thought, as being (to quote W. L. Knox) 'the divine Word or Wisdom, which was at once the divine and living pattern of the cosmos, the

---

[1] R. Reitzenstein, *Das iranische Erlösungsmysterium* (Bonn: A. Marcus and E. Weber, 1921), pp. 105–23; C. H. Kraeling, *Anthropos and the Son of Man* (New York: Columbia University Press, 1927).

[2] See *De Leg. Alleg.* I, 12, 13, and *De Mundi Opif.* 46.

agent by which the cosmos was created, and the divine mind immanent in the cosmos and more particularly in the mind of man'.[1]

The prologue of the Fourth Gospel interprets Jesus' pre-existence in terms of this kind; so does the opening paragraph of the Epistle to the Hebrews; and if Col. 1:15 ff. was written by Paul, it would seem unquestionable that he did, too: 'He [Christ] is the image of the invisible God; his is the primacy over all created things. In him everything in heaven and on earth was created, not only things visible but also the invisible orders of thrones, sovereignties, authorities, and powers: the whole universe has been created through him and for him. And he exists before everything, and all things are held together in him' (N.E.B.). Even those who are sceptical —as I am—of the authenticity of this passage as it stands[2] must acknowledge the signs of essentially the same way of thinking in I Cor. 8:6: 'For us there is one God, the Father, from whom are all things and for whom we exist, and one Lord, Jesus Christ,

---

[1] 'The "Divine Hero" Christology in the New Testament', *Harvard Theological Review*, LXI (1948). Somewhat different is the idea of Jesus as 'Wisdom's prophet' (see J. M. Robinson's article on contemporary German theology in *Interpretation*, XVI, 76–97), which, according to M. Jack Suggs, soon became, in some circles at least, the idea that he was Wisdom herself. Unfortunately, Professor Suggs' important work on this theme has not yet been published.

[2] The Pauline authorship of Colossians is rejected by many scholars; and many others, acknowledging the epistle as a whole to be Paul's, find that it has been subjected to extensive editorial change and interpolation. All of these scholars would be sceptical of Col. 1:15 ff. If any part of Colossians can be regarded as having been written by someone else than Paul, this passage would surely belong to that part. The literature in support of this position is enormous and does not need to be cited here. The same can be said for the more specific argument that the passage is (like Phil. 2:5 ff.; see below, p. 32, n. 2) largely based on an earlier hymn. For a recent and most illuminating discussion of this possibility, with references to the earlier literature, see J. M. Robinson, 'A Formal Analysis of Col. 1:15–20', in *JBL*, LXXVI (1957), 270 ff.

through whom are all things and through whom we exist.'[1]

Yet a third way in which Paul may—again I say, at least sometimes—have conceived of the pre-existent status was as that of an exalted angelic being, doubtless the most exalted of these heavenly persons, and yet specifically neither the Logos nor the Son of Man. This possibility is at least suggested by what appears to be a comparison in Phil. 2:5–11 between the pre-existent Christ and Lucifer (cf. Is. 14:12 ff.). Unlike Lucifer, whose arrogance and ambition led him to try to seize 'equality with God', the pre-existent Christ 'emptied himself', exchanging 'the form of God' for the 'form of a slave'.[2]

All three of these possible ways of understanding how Paul conceived of the pre-existent One can be defended, and perhaps none of them has to be rejected. Such

[1] This meaning of the passage would not be so clearly indicated if it could be shown that Paul wrote δι' ὅν here instead of δι' οὗ. But the textual evidence for the former reading, strong as far as it goes, is too meagre to establish it.

[2] Although obviously I do not favour it, another way of understanding the allusions of this passage must at least be mentioned. Some interpreters see μορφή (form) as a translation of an Aramaic original which meant 'image' or 'likeness' and hold that Paul has in mind here a contrast, not between Christ and Lucifer, but between Christ and Adam, who, also being in the 'image of God', sought to be 'like God' (Gen. 3:5). See J. Héring, Le royaume de Dieu et sa venue (Paris: Libraire Félix Alcan, 1937), pp. 162 f.; also O. Cullmann, The Christology of the N.T., pp. 175 ff, If Paul was thinking in these terms, this passage would be additional evidence for the view that he thought of Jesus in his pre-existence as the Son of Man or as the true and heavenly Man. But the Lucifer analogy seems to me to be much more apt, and therefore more likely. Note that the words 'form of God' and 'form of a slave' are set over against each other in such a way as to suggest a contrast of the most radical and extreme kind, and also that the word ἁρπαγμόν ('robbery') in this passage suggests Lucifer much more readily than Adam. The inclusion of 'under the earth' in verse 10 seems to point in the same direction. Reference will be made below (p. 32, n. 2) to some current discussion of this passage. See also commentaries on Philippians by J. B. Lightfoot, M. Vincent, K. Barth, M. Dibelius, E. Lohmeyer, and·F. W. Beare.

dramatic representations as these, like poetic images generally, can be very different from each other and still be true, even when their subject is the same. They may call attention to different meanings or values in a concrete reality whose total meaning or value is too rich to be expressed in any one of them. But for our purposes in this discussion we do not need to make a decision as among these several possibilities, or even for them all. All we need to do is to observe that Paul undoubtedly affirmed the pre-existence of Christ and that, in whatever more precise terms he pictured it, it was a transcendent, a heavenly, state, far removed in kind from our earthly human existence. I take this, rather than something more particular and specific, to be Paul's meaning when he speaks of Christ as having been 'in the form of God'.

When Paul turns his attention from this pre-existence to the human career, he is apparently aware only of contrasts: Christ 'was rich but for our sakes he became poor'; he exchanged 'the form of God' for 'the form of a slave'; 'he who knew no sin became sin for us'.[1] Nowhere is it suggested that he brought with him any of the glory of his earlier status or that he enjoyed any freedom from the limitations of our human lot or any immunity from 'the sufferings of this present time'. Likewise, when Paul speaks of the earthly career in connection with the post-resurrection life, it is only to point out the stark differences: 'descended from David according to the flesh and designated Son of God in power...by his resurrection from the dead'; 'obedient to death, even death on a cross...therefore God has highly exalted him'.[2] In other words, the sharp corners

[1] II Cor. 8:9; Phil. 2:5-7; II Cor. 5:21.
[2] Rom. 1:3-4; Phil. 2:8-9.

of the (*b*) diagram, presented at the end of the preceding chapter, are still sharp. The human career still stands in stark contrast with the resurrection glory, as it did in the original adoptionism and continued to do for a time, we must surmise, even after a glorious pre-existence had come to be affirmed. Neither end of the diagram nor both ends together have appreciably lifted, so to speak, the middle section.

This 'lifting' of the earthly life nearer the level of both what preceded and what followed it can be readily observed in the Gospels. In Mark, the earliest of them,[1] Jesus appears on the surface to be an extraordinary teacher and prophet, but, at least from the baptism on, he knows himself to be the divine Son of Man. His true nature, hidden from ordinary sight, is sensed at once by the demons and, as a result of miracles and secret teaching, is eventually recognized by the more perceptive of his disciples. And in the other Synoptics, Matthew and Luke, the messiahship is less hidden, and the miraculous confirmation more impressive.

The Fourth Gospel goes much further, reaching the

---

[1] The priority of Mark among the Synoptic Gospels has for so long a time been so widely accepted as, in most critical circles, to be assumed. In 1951, however, B. C. Butler offered a serious defence of the more ancient view that Matthew was the first Gospel (*The Originality of St Matthew: A Critique of the Two Document Hypothesis*, Cambridge University Press), and, more recently, W. R. Farmer in an important work argues that the question of priority should at least be reopened. I must confess to finding what has become the established critical position more probable, but, after reading Dr Farmer's book, I am at least more open to the other possibility. I should say, however, that even if on largely literary grounds a convincing case should be made for the relatively late date of Mark, we should still have to say that at points, at least, that Gospel reflects a more primitive theology than Matthew or Luke. Dr Farmer's book is *The Synoptic Problem* (New York and London: Macmillan, 1964). I should add that nothing of importance for the argument of this book is involved in the way we date the Synoptic Gospels in relation to one another. One may see the 'lifting' we are discussing in each and all of them.

25

point in the operation of this process beyond which (may we not say?) the Church could not have gone without formally embracing docetism. 'We have beheld his glory,' says this writer, speaking of the human Jesus, 'glory as of the only Son of the Father' (1:14). The baptism of Jesus drops from sight as unsuitable to one of his dignity, and even the possibility of temptation is denied. There is no transfiguration scene because the constant glory of the earthly life leaves no room for it. There are indications that Jesus was omniscient and hints, at least, that there were no limits to his latent, but always available, power. It is even suggested sometimes that he was not really susceptible to weariness or hunger or thirst. Certainly he was not subject to changing external circumstances or to the directions or wishes of others. He was always in complete control, not only of what he did, but also of what happened to him. Even his dying was a deliberate act: 'No one takes [my life] from me,' he says, 'but I lay it down of my own accord. I have power to lay it down, and I have power to take it again.' He knew that he 'had come from God and was going to God', and could speak of God's love for him before 'the foundation of the world' and of the 'glory which [he] had with [God] before the world was made', and could say, 'Before Abraham was, I am.'[1]

We cannot for a moment question that John has in mind a genuine human being. No one in the New Testament affirms the reality of the humanity more unequivocally than he: 'The Word became flesh and dwelt among us' (1:14). Indeed, if the Gospel shares to any degree the purposes of the First and Second Epistles of John, one of the writer's aims must have been to refute those who in his own period were denying that Christ

---

[1] John 10:18; 13:3; 17:24; 17:5; 8:58.

had really come 'in the flesh'. But must we not also recognize that in this Gospel, and presumably in the community for which it spoke, the process of qualifying the humanity of Jesus which, under all the conditions, became inevitable once the pre-existence was affirmed, had proceeded as far as it could go short of that formal denial of the human reality which was the final and the intolerable docetic answer?

But Paul largely antedates this development. Not only is it impossible to find in him any tendency to exalt or 'divinize' the earthly life; one must also note that his stress is always on the lowliness and weakness of it. Jesus was 'born of a woman, born under law'. He 'did not please himself'. He became subject to the supernatural 'powers' which for the moment controlled man's life, 'the rulers of this age', who in the end crucified him.[1] Paul 'gloried' in the human life of Jesus just because it was so devoid of glory. Christ 'loved us and gave himself for us' —gave himself in a way absolutely unique: having the 'nature of God' he took the 'nature of a slave'.[2] It would not have seemed desirable to Paul (as sometimes, strangely, it seems to be for us) to be able to say: 'He accepted *to a considerable degree* the limitations and frustrations of our human life,' or 'Being rich, he was willing to share our poverty *to a large extent.*' Such qualifications of Christ's self-giving would have seemed to him both false and faithless. The measure of Christ's humanity was for Paul the measure of the love of God, and there could be no shortening of either. If the love the Church knew in Christ was to be represented by a picture or story (and how else could such love, 'which passes knowledge', be represented?), then it must be the picture or story of a love willing, for our sakes, to

[1] Gal. 4:4; Rom. 15:3; I Cor. 2:6–8.   [2] Gal. 2:20; Phil. 2:5–7.

27

exchange the full reality of the life of heaven for the full reality of the life of earth. No reservation or holding back, at either end, would have seemed tolerable.

There would have been yet another reason why Paul could not consistently have held back, so far as the assertion of the complete and unqualified humanity is concerned: namely, that his whole conception of the 'work of Christ'—by which phrase we mean, I take it, what God purposed and accomplished through him— presupposes the full reality of the human life. This cannot be said of all conceptions of this 'work'. In certain circles, for example, where the salvation in Christ was understood to consist in the possession of an esoteric knowledge which he came to reveal to those capable of receiving it—in these so-called gnostic circles,[1] it was not indispensable that he should have been fully human, or even really human at all. The purpose of the human life

[1] Although the word 'gnosis' (knowledge) gave its name to the kind of religious life and thought here referred to, gnosticism was a complex syncretistic development with many facets. A dualistic world-view— with 'good' spirit set over against 'evil' matter—was perhaps its basic characteristic. Explanations of how God could be related to such a world and of how one might get free of it and thus be saved had in various systems an almost infinite variety. But in all of them salvation is possible through a saving knowledge vouchsafed through a supernatural revelation to an elect *élite*. Many of the New Testament documents—notably, the Pastoral and Johannine Epistles, Jude and II Peter, possibly Colossians— indicate the presence of this kind of teaching in the environment of the Church in the early second century and even before, as well as the vigour of the Church's opposition to it. This struggle is carried further in the work of some of the early Fathers, from whose refutations of the several gnostic systems much of our knowledge of gnosticism has been derived. But we are by no means entirely dependent on these orthodox Christian sources, especially now, since the discovery in 1945 of many gnostic documents at Nag-Hammadi in Egypt. For an admirable selection of source materials representative of this kind of thought, so important a part of the background of the early Church's theology, see R. M. Grant, *Gnosticism: a Source-Book of Heretical Writings from the Early Christian Period* (New York: Harper and Row, 1961).

was to give sensible form to something otherwise un-knowable by men, to express in a way visible and audible on the human plane the eternal Word or Wisdom of God. It was not necessary, then, that Christ should have *been* human; it was enough that he should have *appeared* as such.

Those belonging to such circles we have already re-ferred to as docetists, or 'seemists'; and undoubtedly a part of the explanation of how it happened that the Fourth Gospel could go as far as it did in this direction lies in the fact that its author apparently shared to a degree in their way of understanding the saving signifi-cance of Christ. Jesus was the Revealer. He came that men might 'know the truth' which would 'set them free'. He was 'the light of the world'. 'No one has ever seen God,' this writer says; 'the only Son...has made him known.'[1] I am not suggesting that the Fourth Gospel interprets the saving effect of Jesus' human life solely in this way. Nor do I mean that one who did in fact thus interpret it, even solely and consistently, must needs have been a docetist; only, that such a one might or could have been. A denial of the reality of the human-ity would have been, for the docetist, entirely compatible with the acknowledgement of the salvation in Christ. But, for Paul, this would not have been true.

For Paul saw as the purpose of the Incarnation, not the exhibiting or revealing or making known of a *truth*, but the doing of an *act*. Man's need was not to *see* something, but to have something *done* for him. Paul conceived of this human need in two ways: one, in legal and forensic terms, answering to the fact of man's guilt; and the other, in more concrete and pictorial terms, answering to the reality of his bondage. The same point—namely,

_____
[1] John 8:31; 9:5; 1:18.

29

that something needs to be done, and not merely dis-
closed—can be made in both cases.

As for man's guiltiness, it was not, for Paul, a state of
mind which could be corrected by some fresh vision of
the truth. Nor was it an alienation from God which only
a new attitude on man's part was needed to remove. Such
subjective or largely psychological understandings of our
estrangement from God are not to be found in Paul.
Something more, and other, than a change of heart *in us*
is required if we are to be reconciled. This is why Paul
says nothing about repentance and why he does not find
the term 'forgiveness' important and relevant in this
connection. Our sin, even when understood in this guilt-
producing sense, is not something to be forgiven, but to be
compensated (or atoned) for, or to be dealt with in some
other objective way. Something had to be *done* about it.

The same thing even more clearly appears when we
consider Paul's other, and more characteristic and basic,
way of seeing the human predicament. Man has fallen
victim to evil powers. Sin, a demonic force, has gained
entrance to his existence and has brought him, soul and
body, into a hateful bondage. He is hopelessly enslaved,
utterly unable to break the chains which bind him. His
efforts to extricate himself seem only to strengthen the
hold of his bonds and to deepen his entanglement. Sin
has set him, even against his own will, in opposition to
God's loving purpose for him and therefore in opposition
to the fulfilment of his own true life and the realization
of his own true destiny. He has missed 'the glory of
God', which he was created to share. Instead, he faces
the certainty of final and utter death, which is the fruitage
of sin, the wages with which in the end it pays off its
slaves. He cries out, 'Wretched man that I am! Who
will deliver me...?' (Rom. 7:24). He does not need

enlightenment or gnosis; he needs a more material, more substantial, kind of help; he needs rescuing. Someone must vanquish his enemy and set him free.

And who will this Someone be? Obviously, it will not be a mere man. All mankind, and no less truly every man, is under the dominion of sin and death. Only God can be the Rescuer. Only God can save us. And yet, it would have seemed equally obvious, even God could not do so without entering, in some fashion, into our actual life. For man's enemy was not merely external to him, so that he might be conquered on some super-human field of battle; he was inside. He had established himself *within* human existence. If God was to save us, then, it could not be through an action merely in the cosmic environment of human life, or even an action which only bore or pressed on human life from outside; it had to be an action taking place within it. The enemy had to be met *there* and conquered *there* if he was really to be conquered at all. This meant, as Paul saw it, that God's saving action had to take place in and through a man. As through one man had come sin and death, so through another man must come deliverance and life. As Adam had been truly a man (else how could his disobedience have become the means of our actual bondage?), so Christ must have been truly a man (else how could he have dealt with our actual enslaver?). It would not have done at all to say: 'The Eternal Lord *seemed* to share our actual human life; but, really, of course, he did not.' This sufficed for the gnostic, as we have seen, but such an assertion would have cut the entire ground out from under Paul's theological position.

All of this being true, then, what are we to make of two passages in his letters where he seems to be using the language of docetism? One of these is Phil. 2:7–8: '[He] emptied himself, taking the form (μορφήν) of a servant, being born in the likeness (ὁμοιώματι) of men. And being found in human form (σχήματι) he humbled himself and became obedient unto death, even death on a cross.' We can disregard μορφή, which can better be translated 'nature' than 'form'. But we cannot easily pass by the suggestion of unreality conveyed in ὁμοίωμα and σχῆμα. Perhaps ὁμοίωμα, if it stood alone, could be accepted without too much difficulty: the meaning would have been that the pre-existent One became a man *like* other men. But when Paul adds σχῆμα (the King James Version renders: 'being found in fashion as a man'), he puts an emphasis on appearance or aspect which it is hard to reconcile with a firm confidence in the full and unqualified humanity.[1]

A not implausible explanation can, it is true, be offered. This whole passage (Phil. 2:5–11), it is widely recognized, probably had its original provenance in some Christian group with gnostic and docetic leanings.[2] It comes into Paul's mind at this point in his letter because of the stress it lays upon the humility of Christ (which he wants the Philippians to express in their relations with one another). He no doubt made some changes in it, but he could not, or at any rate did not, eliminate all the signs of its gnostic origin. Among these signs are the words and phrases which have just given us pause.

[1] In the ancient Latin ὁμοίωμα was rendered with *similitudo*, and σχῆμα with *habitus*.

[2] It was, I believe, first suggested, in any influential way, by E. Lohmeyer, *Kurios Jesus: eine Untersuchung zu Phil. 2:5–11* (Heidelberg: Carl Winters, 1928) that Paul is quoting here. The gnostic colouring of the passage is brought out especially by E. Käsemann, 'Kritische Analyse von Phil. 2:5–11', *ZTK*, XLVII, 313 ff. See also J. Jeremias in *Studia Paulina*, ed. J. N. Seevnster and W. C. van Unnik (Haarlem: De Erven F. Bohn, n.v., 1953), pp. 152–4.

Their presence does not mean that Paul found them really congenial or would have used them if, instead of quoting, he had been freely composing.

This explanation is, I can believe, true and relevant up to a point. It *helps* explain. What prevents its being altogether adequate is the presence of a similar phrasing in Rom. 8:2, where there is surely less reason to suspect that Paul is not speaking freely and directly for himself. He speaks there of God's 'sending his own Son in the likeness (ὁμοιώματι) of sinful flesh'. When this passage is considered in connection with the most natural reading of Phil. 2:7–8, I believe we have to recognize the presence in Paul's thought, at least sometimes or in some connections, of a reservation, or misgiving, as to the full genuineness of the humanity of Jesus, which is essentially incompatible with his basic conception of its function or role in God's saving act, as it was also incompatible with that memory of Jesus which belonged deeply and ineradicably to the very being of the Church and in which Paul certainly shared.

Later in this discussion we shall return to these passages and to the contradiction in Paul's thought about the human Jesus which they seem to present.

3

THE POIGNANT DILEMMA

The Epistle to the Hebrews, to which we turn meantime, is an interesting, almost curious, mingling of things new and old and should put us permanently on guard against assuming that the later the date of a document, the less primitive in all respects its teaching will be. On a number of grounds it is hard to find a time for the writing of this book earlier than the nineties, or possibly the eighties, of the first century; and yet its theology has some unmistakably primitive marks. For one thing, the epistle abounds in expressions reminiscent of the original adoptionism. Although the messianic office is conceived of in a fresh way as that of the great high priest, yet, as in the earlier view, Jesus is thought of as having been designated or appointed to this office only after the end of his earthly career and, certainly to some extent, on the basis of what happened in it. He has been 'crowned with glory and honour because of the suffering of death' (2:9). He has gone 'beyond the curtain...as a forerunner on our behalf, *having become* a high priest forever...' (6:20). In a word, the resurrection has here the same crucial significance as in the primitive adoptionism. It was the moment when the man Jesus was 'appointed' the heavenly high priest (5:5).

This point is so important, especially so far as our present inquiry is concerned, and is so often missed that we may appropriately take a little while to confirm and emphasize it. In Hebrews, we are saying, Jesus is represented as having been made high priest *after his death*.

34

I have cited 2:9, 5:5, and 6:20 as all, in effect, saying this. But many other passages affirm the same thing, or at the very least clearly imply it. It is true that Christ is spoken of as having, in his priestly office, 'offered up himself' (7:27), and one naturally thinks of his crucifixion; but it is obvious that the high-priestly offering took place, not on Golgotha, but in the heavenly sanctuary, where after his death Jesus was made the 'minister' of a 'new covenant' (8:1–6). The writer's idea seems to be that although Jesus' actual death provided the material, so to speak, for the sacrifice, the sacrifice itself was offered in heaven (cf. 9:7; 13:11). Jesus was made the high priest only after shedding the blood he was to offer in his priestly office.

It is on this account no doubt that the writer refers so seldom to the resurrection as such (actually, only in 13:20), preferring to speak, in effect, of the ascension. Jesus, we are told, 'passed through the heavens' (4:14); he went into 'the inner shrine behind the curtain' (6:19); he 'entered...into heaven itself' (9:24). It is quite conceivable that the writer, like Paul before him and the most primitive Church in general, did not distinguish between resurrection and exaltation. These were two ways of alluding to the same thing, namely, the fact that the Jesus who was crucified is now Lord and Christ. But, even so, we are bound to be struck by the choice of terms in Hebrews—by the neglect of the idea of the resurrection as such and the almost exclusive preoccupation with what followed it. The explanation is almost certainly the fact that for this writer Christ's saving work was still to be done when he left the tomb, so that the point of greatest significance was not his being 'brought again from the dead' but his entrance into the heavenly sanctuary.

35

But whether or not this is the true explanation of a rather striking peculiarity of the writer's language, the main point is clear: it was after his passion that Jesus became the great high priest, just as, in the more primitive preaching reflected in Acts 2:36, it was after his passion that he was made Lord and Christ. In neither case is any of the glory of his present office and state thought of as attaching to the earthly career. As this writer will tell us again and again, the human Jesus was in all respects a man like ourselves.

And yet it is equally obvious that pre-existence is ascribed to him. This is indicated at numerous points in the course of the writing and at its beginning is unmistakably affirmed. Moreover, this pre-existent state is manifestly being thought of in the most exalted way: Christ in his pre-existence is identified with the heavenly Wisdom or Logos, as in John 1:1–18 and Col. 1:15–17.

In Hebrews, then, we have another instance of a christology in which the pre-existence, being simply added to a previously established pattern, does not seriously alter it. The opening paragraph can serve well to bring out this double and logically contradictory character, an example of that mingling of the new and old to which I have referred as characteristic of this epistle. I shall underline the significant words and phrases, some of which unmistakably reflect the adoptionist picture of Jesus' *appointment* to, or his *entering* upon, his high office, and others, quite as clearly, the view that he was the eternal Logos, through whom all things were made and in whom all things consist: 'In many and various ways God spoke of old to our fathers by the prophets; but in these last days he has spoken to us by a *Son*, whom he *appointed* heir of all things, *through whom* also he *created* the world. He *reflects the glory of God* and bears the *very stamp of his nature, upholding the universe by his word* of power. *When he had made purification* for sins, he *sat down at the right hand* of the majesty on high, having *become* as much superior to angels as *the name he has obtained* is more excellent than theirs.' In a word, we have here another close approximation of the kenoticism which can be surmised to lie between the original adoptionism and the several forms of incarnationism which the New Testament documents represent.

Thus far this character of the Epistle has been discerned chiefly in the significance it accords to the resurrection as the moment of Jesus' exaltation to his messianic office, while at the same time ascribing to him a divine pre-existence. The same combination of terms or images we have observed in Paul. The anomalousness of this combination has been mentioned at a number of points in this discussion, but perhaps it should be emphasized again, before attention is given to another feature of the christology of Hebrews which also belongs integrally only within the adoptionist or the kenoticist picture.

There is, I should think, no need to demonstrate the anomalousness itself. The combination is not a natural or logical one. By this statement I mean only that if christological thought had from the beginning entertained the idea of the pre-existence, it would not have been expected to attribute to the resurrection the kind of meaning that event manifestly had in the primitive preaching. The more fully the logic of the pre-existence is permitted to work itself out in the story, the less important the resurrection is bound to become there. It is not surprising, then, that in the docetic picture it has virtually disappeared. One who, in virtue of who he really was, could not die, could hardly have been raised.

For the same reason, in the Fourth Gospel the

resurrection is no longer the crucial event it still is in Paul and Hebrews. Jesus can say in the prayer before his trial and passion, '[I have] accomplished the work which thou gavest me to do' (17:4), and again, before the ordeal of the cross had ended, 'It is finished' (19:30). The death was a 'departing out of this world to the Father' (13:1), an exaltation, a return to 'the glory which [he] had with [God] before the world was made' (17:5). The resurrection appearances, to be sure, are recorded by John, and they serve to create or confirm faith among Jesus' disciples; but the resurrection itself, far from being the decisive, all-important event it was at first, the very centre and crux of God's mighty act in Christ, now fits smoothly within the continuous story of the divine Son of God, who undertook a mission among men and, having finished it, has returned to his Father, as it was inevitable he should. Earlier I offered some diagrams (see p. 17) to represent the several basic forms of the christological story. Because it is not such a form, what we have called incarnationism cannot so readily be diagrammed; but if we may take the Fourth Gospel as typical, perhaps the following will do:

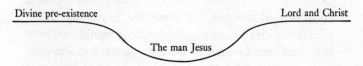

Divine pre-existence   Lord and Christ

The man Jesus

The sharp corners at the end of the first diagram and at both ends of the second are rounded into curves. The divine Logos leaves heaven on an arc which will inevitably return him there!

But how different this is from the original understanding of the resurrection and of the relation in which it stood to the human career which preceded it! That this original understanding could remain intact, even for a little while, once pre-existence was affirmed is surprising and can be explained at all only because the original picture corresponded so closely with the Church's actual experience that it could not immediately be altered, however illogical it might have become after the glorious pre-existence of Jesus, the Son of God, was being proclaimed. Such, we have seen, is the situation reflected in Paul's letters and in the Epistle to the Hebrews.

Before examining how the human career of Jesus is dealt with in Hebrews, I should like to make one other remark about the logic of the pre-existence. If I am right in holding that it was reflection on the resurrection and Jesus' present Lordship which led immediately to the affirmation first of his foreordination to that office and soon afterwards of his pre-existence, then one might reasonably surmise that the first theological problem the early Church faced must have been the problem of *why* the intermediate human life should have been the normal human life it was. No longer, as in the primitive adoptionism, could this normal human life be simply taken for granted. The problem might be stated in some such way as this: If Jesus was really the pre-existent Son of God, we should not have expected his life to be so normal, so free from any hint of his divine status and nature, as we know it to have been. But since it was in fact such a life, there must have been some powerful *reason* for its being such. What was this reason? Why should there have been a human career—and one so fully human as this one was—when, granted its background, one would have expected it to be so shot through with divinity as to be scarcely recognizable as a human career at all?

39

We have already paid attention to the inevitable pressure the pre-existence doctrine exerted on the original picture of Jesus' manhood: Could it have been as normal as it seemed? *Now* I am pointing out that the pre-existence belief really exerted *two* pressures on the early Church's thinking about the human life of Christ— a pressure for *explanation* as well as a pressure toward *modification*—and that the former of these is bound to have been the earlier. The question 'Why should it have been the fully human career it was?' (there being no doubt whatever that it was indeed such a career)— this question, I am suggesting, was asked, and answers were found to it, before doubt of the fact itself was expressed in the question 'Could it really have been the fully human career it seemed to be?' It should also be noted that the two pressures would in a degree have worked against each other. Every *reason* for the humanity which the pre-existence idea forced the Church to find would have confirmed the assurance of its reality which that same pre-existence idea was also working to weaken. And perhaps we can say that, in the ancient Church, the watershed between orthodoxy and heresy with regard to this matter is indicated by the question whether in any given instance the one pressure or the other proved to be the stronger. We have already noted that Paul finds important, decisive *reasons* for the humanity; on this account he must affirm the fact of it. The same thing is perhaps even more clearly true of the writer to the Hebrews.

This writer sees the earthly career of Jesus as an absolutely essential part of his preparation and qualification for the high priesthood for which God had predestined him and on which he entered, as we have seen, after his death and exaltation. This first appears in the second chapter of this epistle, where, after saying that it was 'fitting' that God, 'in bringing many sons to glory, should make the pioneer of their salvation perfect through suffering', he explains *why* it had to be so: '[Jesus] had to be made like his brethren in every respect, so that he might become a merciful and faithful high priest in the service of God, to make expiation for the sins of the people. For because he himself has suffered and been tempted, he is able to help those who are tempted' (2:10, 17–18). The same idea is more elaborately and emphatically set forth in the passage beginning at 4:14 and concluding with the words of 5:8–10: 'Although he was a son, he learned obedience through what he suffered; and being made perfect he became the source of eternal salvation to all who obey him, being designated by God a high priest after the order of Melchizedek.' One notes again that he becomes high priest only after he has 'learned obedience' and has been 'made perfect' and that this happened through what 'he suffered'. His death is the culmination of a preparatory discipline which included his whole life as a man.

This conception of the function or effect of the human career, of the *reason* for it, permits the writer not only to acknowledge its normality without embarrassment but to rejoice in it as a most precious thing. 'We have not a high priest', he writes, 'who is unable to sympathize with our weaknesses, but one who in every respect has been tempted as we are...' (4:15). A little later he is speaking about 'every high priest' when he says, 'He can deal gently with the ignorant and the wayward, since he himself is beset with weakness' (5:1–12); but the context shows that he thinks of this as also true, indeed as pre-eminently true, of Christ. Jesus was 'made like his brethren in every respect' (2:17). In 2:11 the writer goes so far as to affirm that the 'consecrating priest [that is, Christ] and those who are consecrated [that is, his brethren] are all of one stock' (N.E.B.). This comes as near to denying any difference in kind between the human Jesus and ourselves as it would seem possible to come once the pre-existence is asserted. Jesus in his human life stands entirely alongside us. The 'race set before us' was also set before him, and he started it without advantage. He was our 'brother' and we should be no more embarrassed to think of him so than he was 'ashamed to call [us] brethren' (2:11). 'Since the children share in flesh and blood, he himself likewise partook of the same nature' (2:14).

What may well be the most moving instance of this writer's realism in conceiving of the human career is his way of thinking about Jesus' religious or devotional life. Here, if anywhere, one would look for something unique in kind. Even if in all other respects Jesus was like us, surely his relations with God must have been of a different order. And yet the writer does not hesitate explicitly and emphatically to deny this. It is 'in the midst of the congregation' that Jesus praises God and, like us, says, 'I will put my trust in him' (2:12-13). 'In the days of his flesh, he offered up prayers and supplications, with loud cries and tears, to him who was able to save him from death [to which he like us was subject], and he was heard [not because he was the unique person he was, but] for his godly fear' (5:7).

Here would seem to be an acceptance of the humanity as complete as in the original adoptionism. The pre-existence doctrine, to be sure, prevents this acceptance from being the naïve, unthinking, thing it was at first, when the earthly career was simply taken for granted.

Here the humanity is being thought of as significant—as intentional, so to speak—as belonging essentially to God's purpose; but it seems just as unqualified and complete. Here, we may well say, we have a closer approximation to what we are calling kenoticism than the New Testament literature elsewhere presents.

I have just spoken of the christology of Hebrews as being a 'close approximation' to a pure kenoticism. At an earlier point in our discussion I described Paul's in-carnationism as 'coming near to being kenoticism'. Why this kind of qualification? What prevents our saying, in each case, 'a clear example of kenoticism'? Undoubtedly, the answer lies partly in the difficulty *a priori* of suppos-ing that the kenotic idea could have survived in the pure form for more than the briefest period in the history of christological development. The paradox involved in the assertion that One who was 'in the form of God' be-came like other men would appear too stark to be toler-ated for more than a moment. However the discontinuity between the pre-existence and the earthly career might be stressed, reflection would have established almost at once, we would suppose, the necessity of affirming some measure of continuity. The heavenly Son of God in be-coming man did not become someone else. In some deep core of personal existence he must have been as a man what he had been before. And since what he had been before was absolutely unique, there must have been something absolutely unique in the nature of his man-hood. As we have had occasion to note a number of times, it is difficult to see how reflection on the pre-existence could have failed to lead to some such conclusion. And therefore it is hard to suppose *a priori* that it had not done so in the case of Paul and Hebrews. One is the more impressed, then, by the almost complete absence of any signs of this conclusion in either case. The emphasis in both writers is on the reality and normality of the manhood.

The picture, however, is not altogether consistent. It will be remembered that when, in the preceding chapter, this point about the humanity of Christ was being made as regards Paul's teaching, attention was called to two passages which seem to refute it or at any rate to call it into question. These are Phil. 2:7–8 (where Christ is spoken of as 'being born in the likeness of men') and Rom. 8:2 (where God is said to have sent his Son in 'the likeness of sinful flesh'). We noted that, since the first passage is probably largely a quotation, the second is the more important in determining Paul's own position. I ventured then to say that despite the fact that Paul's whole understanding of the saving work of Christ pre-supposed the full and real humanity of Jesus, this word 'likeness' betrays that at times at least he felt some misgiving or reservation. We may now go further and point out that this misgiving or reservation was in connection with the relation in which Jesus stood to *sin*. Paul finds it impossible to say that Christ came 'in sinful flesh', or, to translate more exactly, 'in the flesh of sin'. But since this is the 'flesh' of all other men, does not Paul, by this omission, deny that Jesus fully shared our life?

In Hebrews, one must search harder for any indication of reservation as regards the normality of the humanity. One seems to find it, however, in 4:15, where after saying, 'We have not a high priest who is unable to sympathize with our weaknesses but one who in every respect has been tempted as we are', this writer adds, 'yet without sinning' or, to translate more literally, with N.E.B., 'only without sin'. It is striking that in both Paul and

Hebrews the impulse to draw back from saying, and fully meaning, that Christ was 'like his brethren in every respect' manifests itself at the same point. Despite the violations of the logic of their respective positions which may appear to be involved in the denial, neither writer, when it comes to the test, can bring himself to say that Jesus participated in man's sinfulness. No one will be surprised at this. Who is ready to refer to Jesus as a sinner? We shrink with a kind of horror from even the suggestion of such a thing.

This repugnance is to be accounted for, in considerable part, by the impression the goodness of Jesus has made on us; and, in so far as this is true, is different only in degree from the aversion we might feel to using the same term in other particular cases. The fact of the matter is that although we are forced to know the reality of man's sinfulness in ourselves, we are not in the same inescapable way made aware of it in others. Only when overt manifestations of it force it on our attention are we likely to think of it at all. Thus we do not naturally think of the 'saints' in our acquaintance, the truest and most truly loving persons, as 'sinners'. But if we hesitate to use such language in speaking of a friend, how much more difficult to speak of Jesus so! His goodness was such as apparently to leave no room for the possibility of sin. Here grace and truth seem perfectly united; here we see expressed the full integrity and the utter abundance of love. This is not a mere idealization, an image we have created out of our own searchings and gropings for the good. This character of Jesus is exhibited in the Gospels and, even more important, it belongs to the deepest and most intimate memory of the Church. Here, we cannot but affirm, was a unique human goodness, 'the highest, holiest manhood'. How difficult, then, to think of him as knowing in any sense or degree the taint of sin!

This psychological consideration is enforced by another. The conception of Jesus as Saviour may seem entirely to preclude such a possibility. How, we may ask ourselves, could he have saved if he had stood in any need of being saved? How could he have healed if he had needed healing? How could he have been the means of freeing us from sin if he himself had not been free from it? In even the simplest, the most elementary or most primitive, picture of the Christ, Jesus is *obedient*. And this must mean perfectly obedient; otherwise, how could he be the means of reconciliation for those who through disobedience are estranged from God, from their brethren, and from their own true selves? I am sure I do not need to say more to make understandable the fact that both Paul and the writer to the Hebrews are unable in the last resort, for all their stress on his humanity, to ascribe to Jesus participation in our human sinfulness. They can think of him as sharing in our weakness, but hardly in our sickness.

Let us not fail to note, however, how close both writers come to saying even this. I think it is true to say that each comes as close as he could conceivably come without saying it. Is more than a hair's breadth of separation involved when the writer to the Hebrews speaks of Jesus as being 'in every respect tempted...as we are'? To be sure, the Greek word translated 'tempted' can mean, very generally, 'tried' or 'put to the test', and does not need to mean 'enticed to evil'. But in the present passage, this last meaning, the ordinary meaning of the English word 'tempted', seems clearly indicated.

When the author adds 'only without sin', he does not think of himself as qualifying his earlier statement. But is he not in fact doing so? He means, of course, that Jesus, when he was tempted, did not *consent* to sin, did not succumb to its enticements. But, we may ask, can temptation be real if sin itself is not in some sense or measure already present? Is not sin the presupposition or precondition of temptation even when our resistance or God's grace keeps it from being, in overt act, its consequence? Am I really tempted if I do not, however briefly or tentatively or slightly, consent? Have I been really tempted if I have rejected only that which entirely repels me or that from which I stand entirely aloof? Can we, then, think of Jesus as tempted—and moreover tempted in all respects as we are—and yet as not knowing from within the existential meaning of human sinfulness? I am not now saying that we cannot; I am saying that there is no obvious way in which we can.

Considering still the writer to the Hebrews, one cannot fail to notice also his silence at a crucial point in the definition of Jesus' qualifications for the high priesthood in 5:1–10. The writer is drawing there an analogy between 'every high priest' and Christ as the supreme high priest. He does so by making three points about the ordinary high priest and then showing that they all apply to Jesus in a heightened sense. First, the ordinary high priest is appointed to mediate between God and men. Secondly, 'he can deal gently with the...wayward, since he himself is beset with weakness [and]...is bound to offer sacrifice for his own sins as well as for those of the people'. And, thirdly, he 'does not take the honour, on himself, but he is called of God, as Aaron was'. Having made the three points about the usual high priest, the writer, taking the points in reverse order (an instance of chiasmus), applies them to Christ. In vv. 5–6 he is showing that 'Christ did not exalt himself to be

47

made high priest' but was appointed by God; and in the moving passage vv. 7–8 he is saying that just as the ordinary high priest can be effective only because he is 'beset with weakness', so 'in the days of his flesh Jesus offered up prayers and supplications, with loud cries and tears, to him who was able to save him from death' and 'learned obedience from what he suffered'. It is only because he has thus been 'made perfect' that he can be spoken of (in vv. 9–10) as having become 'a high priest after the order of Melchizedek' and 'the source of eternal salvation to all who obey him'. The author passes over in silence what seem to be the implications of his earlier reference to the priest as offering sacrifice for his own sins as well as for those of the people. I do not want to exaggerate the importance of this silence; but its possible significance is made at least a little more probable by what the writer says in 7:26–8: 'Such a high priest does indeed fit our condition—devout, guileless, undefiled, separated from sinners, raised high above the heavens. He has no need to offer sacrifices daily, as the high priests do, first for his own sins and then for those of the people; for this he did once and for all when he offered up himself' (N.E.B.).

One must also note in this connection the many passages in which this same writer emphasizes the dynamic, growing, developing character of Jesus' goodness. He is now, to be sure, the perfect person (7:26), as indeed the perfect high priest would need to be; but it is unmistakably implied that this has not always been true. His present 'perfection' has obviously been *bestowed* or *acquired*. He 'has been made perfect', we have just read (7:28); so also in 5:9 and 2:10. And although this perfection is not to be understood simply, or even principally, as ethical goodness, surely such goodness is included in it (note, for example, 7:26). So we are also told that he 'learned obedience' (5:8). And since both the learning of obedience and the being made perfect took place through 'suffering', which must mean pre-eminently the cross, we are left to infer that the goodness of the earthly, human Jesus, for all its supreme excellence, was yet the characteristic goodness of a man. Such goodness is never moral perfection in some absolute sense, and in the nature of the case cannot be.

Nor can the fact that Jesus is said to have offered as high priest the perfect sacrifice (9:14) be appealed to as evidence that this writer is thinking of Jesus' earthly life as possessing this perfection. For, as we have seen, it is in the heavenly sanctuary, whither Christ went after his death, that he 'offered himself without blemish to God'. The willing suffering of death was the culminating element in the qualifying, not only of the priest, but of his offering as well.

The point I have been trying to make in all this is that while this author to the Hebrews cannot bring himself to speak, or even to think, of Jesus as a sinner (any more than we can), nevertheless his whole understanding of the story of the Christ and of the role of the human Jesus in it logically requires that the latter should have shared completely in our human lot—without any reservation at all, even this one.

The same poignant problem confronts Paul, and, it would appear, even more clearly and inescapably. For in his form of the story, the whole purpose of God's sending his Son or of the Son's coming was in order that actual contact with sin should be made. Sin had established itself within the flesh and contaminated the whole of man's existence. Christ, it would seem to follow, must come into that very existence if he would deal with man's enemy. And not infrequently Paul says, in effect, that he did just this. What else does he mean when he writes: 'We know that Christ being raised from the dead will never die again; death no longer has dominion over him. The death he died he died to sin, once for all...' (Rom. 6:9–10)? Could he have died to sin without ever having known it? Here again we see the same logical impasse emerging as in Hebrews: any adequate representation (story or picture) of the saving work of Christ seems to require both that we deny to him any part in sin and yet that we ascribe to him a complete sharing in our human life—and, one must add, in that life as involving, most particularly, sin and its consequences.

I have spoken of the problem as being a poignant one. And so it was, we must suppose, for both writers. It should be recognized, however, that it would have been somewhat less disturbing for the writer to the Hebrews than for Paul because the former conceived of sin in a different and less radical way. For the author of Hebrews sin meant primarily sinning—conscious, deliberate acts of disobedience or unfaithfulness. All men, to be sure, were guilty of these sinful deeds; but it would have been at least conceivable that a particular man might refuse to commit sin and thus be free of it. This being true, the assertion of Jesus' sinlessless, although it could not avoid having the effect of qualifying that complete sharing with us which this writer is concerned to emphasize as belonging necessarily to the preparation of the great high priest, nevertheless did not strike at the basic reality of the humanity as such. But Paul had a harder problem. For him sin was not primarily a way of referring to conscious and deliberate acts of disobedience or rebellion on the part of individual men, but was rather a way of designating something in the actual nature of mankind itself.

Man, made in the image of God, had 'fallen'. God's good creation had been despoiled, as by some cruel enemy; hurt and crippled, as by some terrible accident. Could one have shared in that existence and not participated in this wrongness? Paul would have found this question almost impossibly difficult.

It is because of this difficulty, I suggest, that the quasi-docetic language we noted earlier occurs in Paul. Sin for him belongs so inseparably to actual humanity, to 'the flesh', that he cannot conceive of Jesus as being at the same time both sinless and human—that is, he cannot make both points simultaneously and with the same emphasis. If, then, in a given context he seems required to assert that Jesus came 'in *sinful* flesh' (as in Rom. 8:2), he finds himself introducing, perhaps without intending to or even knowing that he was doing so, a hint of the flesh's unreality. He cannot say, in forthright fashion, with the author of the Fourth Gospel: 'The Word was made flesh.' For he sees no way of saying 'Christ came in the flesh' without saying, in effect, 'sinful flesh'. And this he shrinks from saying. And so he finds himself speaking of its 'likeness'.

We do not need to suppose that he used this word 'likeness' with full seriousness, or that, if challenged, he would not have insisted with vehemence on the unqualified reality of Jesus' human existence. He would have recognized, when thus challenged, that if this reality were given up, his whole conception of God's saving work in Christ would have to be abandoned. For what good would it have done us, from Paul's point of view, if God had sent his Son into a 'flesh' which looked very much like ours, but really was not ours? And would it have been any better, as Paul would have seen it, to say that the flesh Christ took *was* our flesh except in one respect: there was no sin in the flesh he took. For why, in that case (Paul would logically have asked), did he need to take it at all? Was not the whole reason for the Incarnation the making possible of an actual encounter of God with sin and death? But though Paul is able without equivocation to acknowledge that the humanity of Christ was mortal, he finds it impossible to say in any clear and forthright way that it was also sinful, in the sense in which all actual humanity, it would seem, must be recognized as being.

Here we have, poignantly focused, the dilemma of early Christian thought about the humanity of Jesus, and indeed our dilemma still: How could Christ have saved us if he was not a human being like ourselves? How could a human being like ourselves have saved us?

4

PRE-EXISTENCE AND HUMANITY

Thus far, except for a little while at the very beginning, we have been engaged almost entirely with the most ancient *story* of Christ in its several forms, with what I have called the primitive Christian mythology. We have seen that although, given the realized values in the early Church's existence and all the conditions of its life, it was inevitable that the primitive adoptionism should have proved inadequate, yet the way of repairing the lack which the community adopted (probably the only way it could have adopted), namely, the assertion of Christ's pre-existence, placed a strain, so to speak, upon the humanity of Jesus which it was unable to bear. In docetism, the manhood is simply denied. In the Fourth Gospel it is, in the formal sense, unambiguously and strongly affirmed, but, in actual fact, has been so transformed by the divinity surrounding it on all sides, as it were, as no longer to be manhood in any ordinary sense. Even Paul and the writer to the Hebrews, each of whom has a motive for maintaining the full integrity of the humanity which John does not have—even they cannot do so without some equivocation and compromise.

In other words, although the early Church always knew that it could not express the truth revealed in its own life without affirming the full reality of both the humanity and divinity of Christ and therefore had no hesitancy in rejecting docetism, nevertheless it found itself unable to accept, simply and consistently, either of what would appear to be the only other possibilities, namely, adoptionism and kenoticism. So much by way of an historical survey which was itself summary and all too brief.

Do I dare now to go beyond such an historical statement and raise the question of actual truth—truth for us, truth for the Church? A systematic, not to say adequate, answer to that question would call for a learning and a competence I do not have. But the question itself rises inevitably out of our reflections on the biblical materials we have been considering, together with some hints, at least, of the direction in which an answer may be sought. I am hoping only to follow out some of these hints as I ask: how are *we* to think of Jesus' humanity and of its place within the total meaning of Christ? The rest of this essay will be concerned primarily with this contemporary question.[1]

We should begin our attempt at an answer by recognizing again the fact, to which attention was called at the very beginning of this discussion, that the terms 'humanity' and 'divinity' as applied to Christ answer basically, not to ideas or thoughts *about* him, but to the Church's experience *of* him. There is a divine and a human ingredient in the concrete reality of Christ. The Church's memory of Jesus is the memory of a man, a *human* being;

[1] A summary discussion such as that on which we now embark cannot hope to deal, even summarily, with all that has been written in modern times on the christological problem. The range of my own reading, certainly more limited than I might wish, will be fairly well indicated by the footnote and other references I shall make. A reader interested in being introduced to the literature of christology in our own period cannot do better than to consult W. N. Pittenger, *The Word Incarnate* (New York: Harper and Brothers, 1958). Most important works are there not only cited but also illuminatingly described and evaluated. Needless to say, many books which have been generally helpful to me, even very helpful, happen not to require citation in the rather meagre footnotes of this book.

its knowledge of the risen, living Lord is the knowledge of a *divine* being—still human, in a sense, since he is still the same being, but now *divinely* human. In other words, the humanity and divinity of Christ are actually fully present, concretely known, realities. It is simply a fact about us as Christians that we both look *back* to Jesus and look *up* to him. He meets us in our memory of him and in our present life with him. But the one we know in memory is fully human; the one we know in worship is *this same one* divinely exalted. Thus, actually to find the humanity and divinity of Christ, not as abstract ideas but as existential realities, the Christian needs only to look into his own heart; and the Church has only to be itself in order to know both. This comes out clearly in the liturgy of the Holy Communion, which is both a remembering of the human Jesus and a receiving of, and communing with, the divine Lord.

It is also important to recognize that the acknowledging of this humanity and divinity of Christ, both in a full, unqualified sense, involves no necessary logical contradiction. We have seen that this was true of the Church's first christology, which was hardly more than the making of this acknowledgement—hardly more than its assertion that what was true in its own experience was also objectively or 'really' true. The one it remembered as a man *had been* a man; the same one was now known as Lord and Christ because he *had in fact been made* Lord and Christ. This was, to be sure, a marvellous, an almost incredible, fact—nothing less than the miracle of the resurrection—but no *logical* difficulty was involved. Nor is there still, so long as we stay close to the primitive and essential *experience* of Christ. There is no reason why we need to say *either* 'Since I know him as divine, he could not have been really human' *or* 'If he was really human,

I must be mistaken in knowing him now as divine'. Neither of these statements is either necessary or true. As present in our memory of him he is human; as present in our total knowing of him he is also divine. The resurrection is our way of referring to, *and objectively accounting for*, this fact in the concrete existence of the Church.

So long, then, as the story is told in this way, it is hardly a story at all (in any mythological or quasi-mythological sense), but is simply a statement of fact. Moreover, one very important matter of fact—namely, the human Jesus who fully shared our life—could be expressed in it with a freedom and consistency hardly possible in any other story form. But more, even than this, can be said for this simplest and most primitive story: one must acknowledge also that it dealt faithfully with all the Church really *knows* of Christ. For the reality of Christ is actually grasped, or actually grasps us, not otherwise than as the remembered Master and the living Lord. However appropriate, or even necessary, the affirmation of it may seem to be, his *pre-existence* cannot, in the nature of the case, be thus *known*.

But if this is true, we may well ask whether the affirmation of it is essentially, or in principle, necessary. Do we need to require more of a christology than that it take adequate account of the experience of the Church? Because I am sure we do not, I believe it can be said not only that the most primitive christology—what we have been calling 'adoptionism'—is the minimally essential christology but also that in its basic structure it was, and might conceivably have continued to be, an entirely adequate christology.[1]

---

[1] I find most interesting in this connection the following words from K. Rahner, S.J., *Theological Investigations* (Baltimore: Helicon Press, 1961), I, 155 f.: 'Let no one say that nothing more is really possible in this field any longer [the field of christology]. Something is possible, be-

This last statement, especially in view of the further christological developments which actually took place, is bound to seem questionable, if not obviously untrue; and I must make some effort to explain and defend it. Under what conditions could the primitive adoptionism conceivably have proved adequate? The answer, in a word, is: things could have worked out so (again I would say 'conceivably') if the centre of interest in the Church's christological reflection had continued to be (as it was at first) an event rather than a person. There is no question that the word 'Christ', whether then or now, designates both a person and an event and that both meanings are always present whenever the term is used. But in any given context the one category or the other may be dominant, and a quite different course of speculation is opened up if one asks 'What was *happening* in Christ?' than if one's question is 'Who *was* Christ?' It was inevitable that both questions should be asked. But it was

cause something *must* be possible, if it is a matter of the inexhaustible riches of God's presence with us and if we honestly admit that we often find traditional Christology difficult to understand...and so have questions to put to its source, the Scriptures.

'For example, let us take so central an assertion of the Scriptures as the statement that Jesus is the Messias and as such has become Lord in the course of his life, death and resurrection. Is it agreed that this assertion has simply been made obsolete by the doctrine of the metaphysical Sonship, as *we* recognize it and express it in the Chalcedonian declaration and that its only real interest for us now is historical...? Is the Christology of the Acts of the Apostles, which begins from below, with the human experience of Jesus, merely primitive? Or has it something special to say to us which classical Christology does not say with the same clarity?...It does indeed follow from the Incarnation of the Word of God through Mary (in the Chalcedonian sense) that he is the "Mediator" between us and God, *provided*, of course, that the real initiative, in some true sense, of the man Jesus with regard to God is given its *genuine* (anti-monothelite) meaning, and Christ is not made into a mere "manifestation" of God himself and ultimately of him alone...Such a "Mediator" would be one in name only.' The whole essay from which this quotation is made, 'Current Problems in Christology', is marked by profound and imaginative insight and repays careful study.

57

not so definitely determined in advance which of them would become the more important in the developing theology of the Church.

In the very beginning, as we have in effect said several times, the basic or dominant christological question was the former of these, the question about the event. We should expect this to be true, for the beginning was a Jewish beginning, and it was natural for the Jew to think of God as manifesting himself in history, or in the world of men, not as a personal presence, not in a theophany as in the pagan mythologies, but in his mighty acts. The God who made known his ways to Moses, his acts to the children of Israel, had now, these primitive Christians believed, acted in a final and supremely sovereign way for the judging and the saving of the nations. This action had taken place in and through the man Jesus, whom God in his foreknowledge had appointed for this mediating task and whom he had raised from the dead as a testimony that it had been accomplished. As a matter of fact, the very name 'Messiah' or 'Christ', which they found themselves giving him, calls attention primarily to the eschatological *event*. The term does not refer to the nature of a person but to a function to be performed by someone (whether human or divine) in the course of God's saving and judging action.

It is always rash to predict what might have been, but surely it is conceivable that if the Christian movement had remained in its original Jewish environment during the years when its theological and credal formulations were taking shape, the Church's christology might have remained in its basic structure what it began as being: 'This same Jesus God has made both Lord and Christ.' And if things had worked out thus, who will say that the structure would not have been adequate?

58

Imagine, if you will, that this was in fact the situation and that it was this comparatively simple christology which the New Testament and the early Fathers had bequeathed to us. To what element in the Church's actual experience of Christ would one be able to point as having been omitted or passed over? His genuine humanity would have been acknowledged without question, complication, or reservation of any kind; the resurrection, his divine Lordship and his presence in (or as) the Spirit would have been fully recognized; and in the assertion that the God of all nature and of all history was, in a unique and absolutely crucial sense, back of, present in, and acting through, the event of which his life was the centre, the human Jesus' supreme and illimitable significance would have been fully confessed and affirmed.

In appropriating such a statement and making it our own, would we not be saying in effect what we say now: that Jesus' human career was the locus of an incomparably significant divine action; that the reality of God himself, 'very God of very God,...came down from heaven' and was manifested, in mighty power, in an event which happened in and through and around this man and was embodied in a community which came to exist, and still exists, in and through and around this same man, raised from death and exalted? Is not this what we actually say, and what, given the nature of the Church, we could not help saying? And if we had inherited directly from the earliest Church this earliest creed, would we have felt the need to say more? What more could have been said? Would we have felt the need of giving to Jesus some higher status? What higher status could we have given him?

As a matter of fact, however, the Christian movement

did not long remain in its original Jewish environment, and even if it had, one cannot be sure the christological question would not eventually have taken the alternative form, the centre of interest shifting from the divine meaning of an event to the divine nature of a person. At any rate, this change did in fact take place. Not that there ceased to be a sense of the *event*, a realization that something of crucial significance had *happened*; this awareness persisted and persists still. But the shift occurred as the Church reflected on the source or cause of this significance. Was the event significant because of what God did or because of what Jesus was? The original answer, as we have seen, was undoubtedly the former. The eventual answer tended more and more to be the latter.

The change began when, very early indeed, the pre-existence of Christ was first affirmed. This affirmation, to be sure, did not at the very outset modify the primitive adoptionist pattern or change the earlier almost exclusive emphasis on God's dynamic action in raising Jesus from the dead and making him Lord and Christ. But this would have been true for only the first brief unreflective moment. Almost at once, the locus of interest would have begun to shift. One would have asked: who and what *was* this person in his pre-existent state, and therefore who and what was he 'really'? It was unthinkable that, in answer to this question, his nature and status should not have been defined in the highest conceivable terms; and, given the prevalence in both Jewish and Hellenistic circles of the idea of Wisdom or Logos, it was all but inevitable that the pre-existent Christ should very soon have come to be identified with this divine hypostasis and thus to be thought of as participating in the reality of God himself. It was this heavenly Person who had become a man—and become a man without really ceasing

to be the heavenly Person he was (indeed, how *could* he?).
Or, the same thing said conversely, Jesus as the particular individual he was had existed before all worlds.
And the 'mystery' of Christ—that is, the secret explanation of what had happened to bring the new Creation into
being—lay no longer primarily in God's having acted
as he did, but in Jesus' having been what he was.

Now I do not think we can hope for a clear christology
of our own until we recognize the distorting nature of
this development—natural, even inevitable, though it
may have been. It involves, whether we want it to or not,
a denial of the full reality of the humanity of Jesus and
therefore strikes at something essential in the nature of
the Church. Each part of this double statement can be
seriously challenged. One may ask: 'Does it need to be
said that the identification of Jesus in his personal
existence with the pre-existent Logos implies a denial of
his humanity?'; and then raise the further question,
'Even so, how does such a denial violate anything
essential in the Church's existence?' To the second of
these queries we shall give our attention in the following
chapter. We must now give some consideration to the
first of them.

It will be recognized at once that the formal answer the
Church—that is, the Church as a whole, the catholic or
orthodox Church—has given to any questioning of the
actuality of Jesus' humanity has invariably been a firm
No. We have observed this answer in the Fourth Gospel:
'The Word became flesh.' And the same answer, even
more explicit and vigorous, is found in the Fathers and
in the ancient Creeds. But, as we know, there are, in the
case of words no less than with other things, ways of
taking back with one hand what one has just given with

the other. One may affirm the humanity as a formal fact and then proceed so to define or portray it as to deny its reality in any ordinarily accepted sense. This, we have already noted, is true of the Fourth Gospel. The author's assertion (or assertions) of the manhood can hardly avail against the effect of his portrait of an essentially divine person.

The same thing, I should say, is true of the Fathers. Norman Pittenger has written: 'In my judgment a fundamental difficulty with the Christology of the patristic age is that while in word it asserted the reality of the humanity of Jesus Christ, *in fact* it did not take that humanity with sufficient seriousness. Excepting for those like the Ebionites and like such condemned "heretical" theologians as Paul of Samosata, the tendency of Christological thinking in the mainstream of what was believed to be "orthodox" was far more heavily weighted on the side of the divinity than of the humanity in Jesus. This was not, of course, true of the Antiochene school, but the influence of that school did not really have the effect that one might wish it to have had; and "orthodox" Christology, even when the excesses of Alexandrine teaching were somewhat restrained at Chalcedon in A.D. 451, has tended toward an impersonal humanity, which is, I believe, no genuine humanity at all.'[1] The exceptional character of the Antiochene christology is properly noted. But surely it is true to say that, even for this school, the humanity is qualified or hedged about in a way unique to Jesus; and if this is so, can it be regarded as a fully genuine humanity? Would one even of the Antiochenes have rejected as historically inaccurate such Johannine sayings of Jesus as 'I am the bread of life' (6:35), or 'I am the resurrection and the life' (11:25),

[1] *The Word Incarnate*, p. 89.

or 'I and the Father are one' (10:30), or Jesus' prayer, 'Father, glorify thou me in thine own presence with the glory which I had with thee before the world was made' (17:5). But can we imagine a true man's speaking in any such fashion? And could anyone, be he Antiochene or Alexandrian, ancient or modern, who finds it natural, or even possible, to regard such words as the actual words of Jesus of Nazareth be thinking of him as fully a man? We would surely agree with the comment of Philip Schaff, in connection with the last mentioned of these Johannine passages: 'How absurd would it be for a man to utter such a prayer!'[1]

Schaff, as I understand him, would go on to say at once, 'But, of course, Jesus cannot properly be referred to as "a man". He was "man"—that is, his humanity was a real humanity—but he was not "a man" like other "men".' We may ask, however, whether we can speak significantly of the humanity of Christ unless we *do* regard him as having been 'a man like other men'. Is there any conceivable way of one's being 'man' except by being 'a man'? Many theologians whose integrity and learning I greatly respect have answered that there is. I can only say that I cannot follow them, either in the sense of agreeing with them or of thinking in their terms.

One of the most ancient of these, and undoubtedly the most influential, Cyril of Alexandria, contended, in effect, that Jesus was human in his *nature*, but not in his essential being—in what was called the *hypostasis* or *persona*. This ontologically subsisting element was, in Jesus' case, the Logos, who took a human nature. Jesus' humanity, then, was a genuine humanity; but he himself as a 'person' was the Logos. This way of understanding

[1] *The Creeds of Christendom*, I (New York: Harper, 1884), 33.

how a pre-existing divine being could become an actual human being became orthodox teaching and has dominated the Church's thinking about the 'person' of Christ ever since. One is bound to ask, however, whether 'humanity' without a personal centre which is also human (no matter how the word 'personal' is defined) can properly be called humanity at all. In rejecting the earlier Apollinarianism, the Church would seem to have said that it could not be. But Cyril's doctrine of *anhypostasia* (impersonal humanity), as well as the later adaptation of it by Leontius of Byzantium (*enhypostasia*), is reminiscent of the condemned teaching, to say the very least; and, as many critics point out, the same can be said of the 'christologies' of a number of contemporary theologians who, struggling with the same problem, have found ways (as they suppose) of ascribing to Jesus a real humanity without regarding him as having been a man like ourselves.[1] It is refreshing to hear D. M. Baillie

[1] As writers on christology of whom this may be said, I may mention R. C. Moberly, *Atonement and Personality* (New York: Longmans, Green, 1902), esp. pp. 86 ff.; L. Hodgson, 'The Incarnation', in A. E. J. Rawlinson, *Essays on the Trinity and the Incarnation* (London: Longmans, Green, 1928), pp. 363–402, and *And Was Made Man* (London: Longmans, Green, 1928), esp. pp. 25–7; H. M. Relton, *A Study in Christology* (New York: Macmillan, 1934), esp. pp. 215–35; E. Brunner, *The Mediator*, tr. by O. Wyon (New York: Macmillan, 1934), esp. pp. 328–54; and E. L. Mascall, *Christ, the Christian and the Church* (London: Longmans, Green, 1946), pp. 1–67, and *Via Media* (London: Longmans, Green, 1956), pp. 79–120 (esp. 102 ff.).
These writers have their distinctive ways of stating both the problem and the answer, and I do not want to discount the importance of these differences. At the same time I have no intention of trying either to present or to criticize their particular positions. Nor does my purpose in mentioning them require that I should. My point is only that all of them alike seem to be able to think of Jesus as having been fully and genuinely human without being, in any ordinary sense, a man. Much more competent criticisms than I could make may be found in D. M. Baillie, *God Was in Christ* (London: Faber and Faber, 1948), pp. 85–93; and in W. N. Pittenger, *The Word Incarnate*, pp. 99–111, 132–45. See also N. Ferré, *Christ and the Christian* (New York: Harper, 1958), pp. 73–140;

saying (in a criticism of *anhypostasia* ancient and modern): 'Surely whatever else Jesus was, He was a member of the human race, the human species, a man among men, or one man among others. However true may be the conception of human solidarity, or of the solidarity of Christ with mankind, or of Christ as the "representative Man" through whom we come to God, it remains true that he was a man among men...While to speak of Jesus as "a God" is nonsense from a Christian point of view, it is equally nonsense to say that He is "Man" unless we mean that He is a man.'[1]

I can see, to be sure, that in a non-mythological context it would be more accurate, in speaking of the Incarnation, to say, '...became man', than to say, '...became a man'. But I should insist that, when one thus speaks, one is not referring to the personal existence of Jesus of Nazareth. The reference, whether one consciously understands it thus or not, is to a *social* existence, to human beings in community, to men in their mutuality and interdependence. To say, 'The Word became flesh', is not, most strictly speaking, to say that the Word became 'a man', but rather that the Word became, in a unique and supremely significant way, active and manifest within the life of 'man'; it was thus that he became 'embodied', 'incarnate', in human existence. That this embodiment or incarnation took place specifically in Jesus-as-related-to-his-own, in the new corporate reality (potentially and in principle inclusive of all mankind), the new communal existence, which came into being through him and of which he was the head and heart— not only is it true that the Incarnation can be thus

C. Welch, *The Reality of the Church* (New York: Chas. Scribner's Sons, 1958), pp. 97–112; G. S. Hendry, *The Gospel of the Incarnation* (Philadelphia: Westminster Press, 1958), pp. 83–91.

[1] *God Was in Christ*, p. 87.

specifically identified, but also that 'man' (not 'a man') is clearly the more accurate way to speak of its locus. 'A man' could have been—and was—the means, the agent, the centre, eventually the symbol, of this new Creation, this dynamic 'en-man-ment' of the Word of God, but he could not have been, in his own individual personal existence, the Incarnation itself.

The conception of the Incarnation and of the relation of Jesus to it, which is reflected here, I have set forth with some fullness elsewhere.[1] In gist it is as follows: The Church is the *distinctive* Christian reality. All Christian theology is an effort to explicate and explain the Church's existence and what is found within it. This effort takes the form of a christology—that is, of a teaching about Jesus—because the inner existence of the Church is so fully preoccupied with him, consisting as it does, essentially and all but entirely, in the corporate remembrance of Jesus and the corporate awareness of him as living and present within its life. It is this we mean when we speak of the Church as the 'body of Christ'. And it is because the Church *is* his body and, in history, his only body, that we can often use the words 'Christ' and 'Church' interchangeably, saying 'in Christ' when we are wanting to refer to what it really means to be—and really to be—in the Church. It is this embodiment or incarnation (that is, the Church) which is most immediately—indeed alone is immediately—*known*. The significance of Jesus and the event which happened in and around him is implicit within this known reality. The situation is not that we can speak of the Church as the body of Christ because we have a prior belief in an earlier Incarnation, but rather that we can

[1] Most fully in *The Church and the Reality of Christ* (New York: Harper and Row, 1962; London: Collins, 1963).

speak of the Incarnation at all only because we have been made a part of a 'body', a corporate reality, which *is* Christ in history. The 'earlier Incarnation' was *this* incarnation being brought into being. And so I say again, the Incarnation originally took place, not within the limits of an individual's individual existence, but in the new communal reality, in principle co-extensive with mankind, of which he was the creative centre.

Thus, to recognize the appropriateness of saying that '...Very God of Very God...was made man' (rather than 'a man') is quite compatible with the recognition that the One through whom (and, in a certain extended sense, *in* whom) this incarnation occurred was, and had to be, a man. And to call him a man would mean nothing at all if we did not mean 'a man like other men'.

Because of the importance, and the difficulty, of being understood on this point, I want to state my meaning as clearly as I am able. I should say that the assertion of Jesus' humanity implies something rather definite about his self-consciousness and also about the actual anthropological, biological, and sociological structure of his being. As regards the latter, an affirmation of Jesus' manhood is an assertion that he was born out of, and into, humanity in the same sense every man is; that he was a son of Abraham, just as every man participates in his own race or nation or culture; and, more important, that he was a son of Adam, as all men are, regardless of what their culture, nation or race may be. There is no other conceivable way of being a man. Not only is it impossible, by definition, that God should become a man, it is also impossible, by definition, that he should 'make' one. A true human being could not be freshly created. Such a creation might look like a man and even speak like a man. He might be given flesh like a man's and a man's faculties, but he would not *be* a man. He would not be a man because he would not belong to the organic human process, to the actually existing concrete entity in nature and history, which is, and alone is, *man*.

As to Jesus' self-consciousness, we should be affirming (in our assertion of his manhood) that it was, in its every part and in all of its dimensions, the kind of self-consciousness we find in ourselves and take for granted in other men. Can we imagine Jesus saying to himself, 'I am not a man', or asking himself, 'Am I a man?', any more than we can imagine our entertaining such thoughts about ourselves? Unless he was human to the lowest depths of his conscious and sub-conscious life, he was not truly human at all. He must have learned as we learn and have grown as we grow. His joys must have been human joys and his sorrows the immemorial sorrows of men like ourselves. He must have known loneliness, frustration, anxiety, just as we do. He must have felt temptations to doubt and fear. He would have loved others in the way men love their fellows—more, we shall say, but not differently. He, too, would have shrunk from death, the breaking of familiar ties with beloved things. His knowledge of God, for all its sureness and its peculiar intimacy, would have been the kind of knowledge it is given men to have of their Creator and Father. If all of this were not true, would we be able to say that he was truly man? For the real marks of a man are not his shape and appearance, or the way he walks, but the way he feels and thinks in his heart, the way he knows himself, others, and God.

Unless Jesus was a man in such a way as this, could we call him truly human at all? Will we not agree that we could not? Of course, we are likely to add, we shall not find sin in his humanity. So said the author to the

Hebrews and, when it came to the point of having other-wise to say the opposite, Paul as well. Pretty soon it was not necessary to say it; the sinlessness of Jesus was taken for granted. And such is still the case. But unless sin is to be defined in a starkly and exclusively voluntaristic sense and, moreover, is to be associated only with out-ward, overt actions, I should say we cannot make so enormous an exception in Jesus' case without effectively separating him from our humanity. For most of us, I dare say, the word 'sin' cannot be thus defined or limited. If it should be, some other term would be needed to designate the wrongness or perverseness in human existence in which every man is inextricably in-volved. How could one be human and not be implicated in the unjust and often cruel structures of our human world—to some degree consenting to them and to some degree tainted by them? How could one be human with-out knowing the presence of evil in the heart, the poignant reality of temptation? Does not human virtue itself have its distinctive character because this evil is there, to be resisted and perchance overcome?

Indeed, it seems to me that this difficult and sometimes agonizing question about the sinlessness of Jesus could better be put as a question, not about his relation to sin at all (though a certain relation is surely implied), but about the nature of his goodness. Was it a *human* good-ness? Was it, for all its exceptional, even unique, excel-lence, the characteristic goodness of a man? In that case, it was not moral perfection, without weakness or strain or fault or flaw. Define goodness in *that* way, and only God is good, as Jesus himself reminds us (Mark 10:18). Human goodness is born in a struggle with evil—with evil in the environing world and within the heart itself—and is precisely what it is on that account. It is neither impregnable to evil nor unscathed by it. It has its characteristic excellence and beauty only because it bears the scars of battle.

If we should agree that the word 'humanity' has to be defined in some such way as I have indicated, then I believe we should be forced to recognize that the term docetism is much more widely applicable than we usually suppose. For if 'being human' means 'being a man', and if 'being a man' means sharing fully in man's existence (and not merely in some human 'essence'), it follows that if *in any respect* Jesus did not share in that existence, he only *seemed* to be human. D. M. Baillie begins the excellent book to which I have already referred more than once, *God Was in Christ*, with a section headed, 'The End of Docetism'. Citing in it contemporary writers of all schools, he points not only to their explicit repudiations of all formal denials of Jesus' real humanity, but also to the radical and thoroughgoing way in which they accept its full implications. He concludes: 'All serious theological thought has finished with the docetist, Eutychean, Monophysite errors which explained away the humanity of our Lord and thus the reality of the Incarnation. No more docetism! Eutyches, we may say, is dead, and he is not likely to be as fortunate as Eutychus in finding an apostle to revive him! That is the first factor in the distinctive situation of Christology today.'[1]

But having said this, Dr Baillie is apparently unaware of taking any of it back when, only a little later in the same book, he criticizes most sharply—and, I should say, not unjustly—the views of such theologians as Leonard Hodgson and Emil Brunner, saying of the former that 'the Christology which he reaches seems to me to be a

[1] *God Was in Christ*, p. 20.

restatement in modern terms, not of the catholic doctrine, but rather of the Apollinarian heresy', and of the latter: 'All this does, as it seems to me, lead straight to Apollinarianism, if it leads anywhere at all.' Of yet another theologian, L. S. Thornton, he writes: 'His argument...seems to me...to exclude the possibility of recognizing the Jesus of the Gospel story as a real man.'[1] But, one must ask, is not this docetism? By what right do we define that word in such a way as to include Eutyches and altogether to exclude Apollinaris? If we limit the application of it to those who explicitly and formally deny the genuineness of the humanity, perhaps we can do so; but surely that is an arbitrary limitation. Those who formally and explicitly *affirm* the humanity can define it in ways which, in effect, deny its existential reality.

Needless to say, there is no reason *a priori* why we should not define our terms in any way that suits us. We may decide to mean by 'humanity' (where the term is applied to the earthly Jesus) humanity as God intended it and originally created it, humanity as it was before the 'fall', humanity as it ought to be and eventually, in the *eschaton*, will be, humanity as it is in its true nature (whether as created or redeemed). Similarly, we may define this same Jesus' being 'man' in such a way as does not require his belonging, integrally belonging, to the whole process of man's evolution and history, or his sharing, fully sharing, in the self-conscious existence which all other men have known, or his being subject, really subject, to all the limitations of power, knowledge, and virtue which constitute our human finitude or belong inescapably to our existential or 'fallen' estate.

[1] *Ibid.*, pp. 85 ff. Father Thornton's book is *The Incarnate Lord* (London: Longmans, Green, 1928).

As to whether it is possible, or theologically significant, to affirm that kind of humanity of Jesus is a question to which we shall come in the next chapter. At the moment I am concerned only to insist that when we make the affirmation we are not attributing to Jesus the humanity which we know and belong to and which alone has any actual existence in nature or history.

5

HUMANITY AND REDEMPTION

We have seen that from the moment the personal identity of Jesus with the pre-existent Logos (or some other heavenly being) was first accepted as true, the actuality of his existence as a human being like ourselves has been under an intolerable pressure. Manhood, to be sure, has been affirmed of him, but, generally speaking, it has been so amplified, supplemented, or otherwise altered as no longer to be recognizable as the manhood we know. In our formal christologies, however truly 'human' Jesus is alleged to have been according to some chosen, and possibly defensible, definition of that term, he has not been regarded as human in the ordinarily accepted sense, as being a man 'like his brethren in all respects'.

But what about the actual truth of the matter? Was he in fact such a man, or not? Moreover, does it matter whether he was, or not? Or whether we think of him as such, or not? It is to such questions that our discussion has brought us. If it is true that the belief in the pre-existence of Jesus is incompatible with a belief in his genuine normal humanity, then it is clear that an affirmative answer to our questions about the humanity will require some reassessment of that belief. This we shall undertake in the following chapter. Just now I am concerned only to insist that, at whatever cost in terms of other cherished beliefs, the reality and normality of Jesus' manhood must be maintained. If we should find ourselves in the position of having to decide between the pre-existence and a fully authentic human life, there is no doubt what our choice should be. Although it would be a grievous error to suppose that the humanity of Jesus is surer or more important than his divinity—the two are equally sure and equally important—the humanity is both more sure and more important than the pre-existence.

These adjectives 'sure' and 'important' can serve as the organizing terms for the present chapter.

We begin, then, by considering the grounds of our assurance that Jesus was a human being like ourselves. The most obvious and elementary of these—to which we shall give only a moment—is that we should naturally expect him to be. His humanity, that is, his being in all respects a man, is so reasonable a presupposition that the burden of proof lies heavily on anyone who would assert the contrary. An *a priori* consideration of this kind cannot be decisive—the actual facts can sometimes disprove the most confident expectation—but its force is undeniable; and this is true for the Christian believer as surely as for others.

When, moreover, we go on to the actual facts—that is, the data provided by the Gospels and, less explicitly, by other New Testament books—we find that, far from disproving our expectation, they entirely confirm it. What emerges from a critical study of these data is the conception of a normally human Jesus. To be sure, we have seen that in no primitive source is this relatively simple conception consistently presented. But we have also been reminded of the enormous pressures under which that conception would have stood from the very beginnings of the Church's life. The sense of the wonder of the event, expressed almost at once in the assertion of Jesus' pre-existence, and the continuing and ever more intense reflection on its meaning, would have led inevitably to modification of the first simple picture. Even the earliest of the New Testament documents reflects at least a decade of Church history, and we should hardly expect to find there the original picture itself, whole and intact. But, generally speaking, the more primitive the source, the more closely what I have been calling the simple picture is approximated; and, furthermore, vestigial elements of that picture are to be found in all the documents, whether early or late.

We are often warned against arguing in a circle in this matter—against assuming that because a document tends to reflect this simpler conception of Jesus, it is, merely on that account, to be regarded as more primitive, and, conversely, that a 'high' christology is *ipso facto* a late one. The *caveat* is reasonable and salutary, but in this case does not really apply, since the relative dates of the New Testament documents can be established on other grounds as well. It is not too much to say that the disinterested critical reader of the New Testament is almost bound to conclude that, for however short a time —and however rightly or wrongly, adequately or inadequately—Jesus was at first regarded simply and naturally as a man. Many of us would go on to say that if this was the earliest, the most naïve, view, it is also most probably the true one. Eyewitnesses cannot be counted on to see the full significance of the facts they report, and certainly that was true in this case, but they are likely to be the best judges of the facts themselves.

I hope it is not necessary to say that speaking of Jesus as having been 'a man in the ordinary sense of that word' is by no means equivalent to speaking of him as having been an ordinary man. No disinterested historian, with any imagination at all, will arrive at any such conclusion, and I find it hard to understand how certain theologians have been able to speak doubtfully, or even slightingly, of the human greatness. Not only is it true that the qualities of an altogether extraordinary personality are clearly reflected in the Gospel narratives and in innumerable descriptive references elsewhere in the New Testament, but it must also be said that without the assumption that Jesus was such a person it is impossible to understand, in any degree whatever, the historical consequences of his brief career. All of this is fully granted. What is meant by the cited remark is that there is every reason to believe, on the basis of a critical study of the sources, that, however extraordinary he may have been, he was fully subject to the limitations which define and restrict man's life, and that his manhood in the ordinary sense was taken for granted by others and by himself.

So much by way of a very summary statement of the 'objective' case for the normal manhood of the man Jesus. The Church's assurance of his full human reality, however, is not really based on such considerations—certainly is not based on them alone, or even primarily. That assurance rests, rather, on the persistent presence of a certain image within its own life, the image of 'Jesus Christ our Lord'. This image is exceedingly rich and complex, as any study of the terms 'Lord' and 'Christ' will reveal; but an essential constituent of it is a fully and unqualifiedly human 'Jesus'.

I have used the word 'memory' to designate the Church's sense of this actual human person. Many critics have found fault with this term, and I should be the first to agree that it is not ideally suitable. But what better one will someone suggest? It will not do to speak of 'the picture of Jesus as the Christ', as Tillich[1] and others do, unless we are also affirming an element of factual truth in the picture, that is, the actuality of the one pictured. In saying this about the meaning of Tillich's phrase, I am assuming that he is seeking to explicate the life of the Church, an assumption which would seem to be justified by the fact that only within the Church can the picture be seen at all. And *there*, I am saying, it is seen as a *true* picture. The Church not only sees a picture of Jesus, but also, in that same act of vision, knows the picture to be that of an actual person. The picture has no existence except as that kind of picture. Under these conditions perhaps we should say, not that the Church sees a picture of Jesus, but that it sees *him*. Now in ordinary waking life the only place where this kind of 'seeing' takes place is in *memory*. It is there, and only there, that images carry in themselves the assurance of their own factual truth. It is for this reason that the term has seemed to me appropriate, even indispensable, in speaking of the Church's knowledge of the human Jesus. But I have no desire to defend a *word*. My only concern is that the reality I am speaking of be recognized and acknowledged as an essential and inalienable element in the Church's existence.

Now this 'remembered' reality is a fully and unreservedly human reality. The Church does not 're-member' the miracles. It does not, strictly speaking, 'remember' the resurrection; it *knows* the resurrection and has always known it since its birth as the selfconscious community it is, but it does not 'remember' it.[2]

---

[1] P. Tillich, *Systematic Theology* (Chicago: University of Chicago Press, 1957), II, 88–180, *passim*.

[2] The distinction here is not the easiest to draw, and many perhaps will feel that it is unreal. It must be acknowledged that the resurrection could not be really known except in the 'remembering' community, for

What it 'remembers' is a man—a man 'full of grace and truth', but nevertheless a *man*, one whose 'grace' and 'truth' are such as fit the nature of a man. I have said that the Church's image of Jesus as Lord and Christ is extraordinarily complex, with elements human and divine mingled and fused inextricably. The element we are calling the remembrance of Jesus is an integral part of this total image and cannot be separated out of it. But this does not keep it from being the remembrance of a

the obvious reason that the knowing of it was not simply the knowing of a divine Presence, but the knowing of this Presence as the Presence of *Jesus*—and this means the involvement of memory. Still, this is not the same thing as saying that the resurrection itself is 'remembered'. 'The resurrection' is a way of referring to the living Presence of the remembered One, and thus to the reality of the Spirit and to the inner existence of the Church.

The term can also be used, however, to designate an incident in time and place, a temporal occurrence, the moment when Jesus 'arose from the dead'. Not only is it proper to understand the word in this way, one cannot escape the claim of the gospel that this incident actually took place. No process of demythologization which does away with the actuality of this occurrence can be true to the gospel's intention. Moreover, and by the same token, the denial of this actuality is an intolerable contradiction to the Church's existence as the community of Jesus Christ our Lord. For how could Jesus, who was crucified, the remembered One, have become Christ, the living Lord, except through the interposition of some objective occurrence? And how can this 'objective occurrence' be described otherwise than as a 'rising from the dead'. Still, the Church cannot be said to 'remember' this occurrence, any more than anyone could have claimed to have witnessed it and thus to be in position to describe its phenomenological character. The first Christians saw the risen Jesus (and there can be no doubt that they did!), but not his rising. Their assertion that he had risen was an inference from their knowledge of him as both remembered and living. And so it must always be. This does not mean that the assertion is of doubtful truth. On the contrary, it is an inescapable implication of the Church's existence.

No one has dealt more authentically and more creatively with the problem of the historical meaning of the resurrection than has R. R. Niebuhr in *Resurrection and Historical Reason* (New York: Charles Scribner's Sons, 1957). This book has the great merit of recognizing that the resurrection *occurrence* is being affirmed whenever the resurrection in any Christian sense is being confessed, of seeing the great difficulties, especially in our modern period, of finding a place in history for such an occurrence, and of proposing a viable way of doing so.

truly human person. We could not think of him as our Lord *in the distinctive way we do* if we did not also think of him as having been our brother. We could not think of him as sharing the life of heaven *in the particular way the Christian does* if we did not think of him as having first known all the limitations and imperfections of man's earthly existence. He could not be the *divinely* human Lord we know him now to be if he had not been the *humanly* human Companion we remember him to have been.

In the preceding chapter I ventured to say that a denial of the full humanity of Jesus 'strikes at something essential in the nature of the Church'. In making this remark I had principally in mind precisely this 'remembrance' of him as a constituent element in the actual being of the Church. This concrete knowledge of the human Jesus appears unmistakably in the Church's prayers and hymns, however obscured it may sometimes be in its theologies or creeds. Indeed, it was the importance of this concrete knowledge, rather than any merely theoretical or theological considerations, which made inevitable the Church's rejection of all overt or explicit docetism. Actually, however, any authentic attempt at coherent rational explication, or theological explanation, of what is given in the Christian existence has as much need of the assumption of Jesus' genuine humanity as does the life of Christian devotion itself. It is important to consider just why this is true.

It will be recalled that in our discussion of the primitive christology, the point was made that an almost inevitable drive toward docetism in the Church's thinking about the 'person' of Christ was in a measure countered or checked by its ways of thinking about his 'work'. Where this work was conceived of as purely revelatory, as being

79

simply and only the disclosing of a saving truth, as in various forms of gnosticism, there was nothing to prevent the tendency from following its course to the end; on this account, as well as for other reasons, the gnostic christology is always docetic. What proved to be the authentic Church, however, refused to settle for any such conception of Christ's work. We have seen that Paul finds the meaning of Jesus' earthly life in a way of dealing with sin and death. The writer to the Hebrews understands it both as a necessary precondition of Jesus' becoming the great High Priest and also as a necessary element in his preparation for that office. For neither writer would a mere 'appearance' have had any significance or value at all. The situation, it was pointed out, was not that men needed to be *shown* something to be saved, but rather that something needed to be *done* for them, something which could be done only by, or in, or through, a man. Even the Fourth Gospel, although it went a long way in the gnostic-docetic direction and speaks constantly of Jesus as the one who saves by enabling men to 'see' or to 'know', nevertheless refuses to allow that his saving work can be fully or exhaustively described in these terms and thus at the crucial point rejects the docetic conclusion.

Now these ancient ways of describing the work of Christ belonged to imaginative constructions which can hardly be taken as literally accurate accounts of actual happenings or transactions. We know we are speaking metaphorically, at least in part, when we call Jesus the great high priest, or refer to him as a lamb sacrificially slain for the expiation of our guilt, or as a mighty benefactor paying a ransom for our release from slavery to sin and death, or as a conqueror meeting and destroying these same enemies. Probably, too, the biblical writers themselves were to some extent aware that they were using metaphors. The obvious disparateness and contradictoriness of the images which even the same writer might employ would seem to indicate as much. But underneath, supporting, and expressed in these several ways of speaking was the conviction that in Jesus and the event which happened through and around him, mankind was being given not merely a new vision of God or a new insight into the truth about him but rather God's own presence and mighty action in and among us, in our actual history, defeating our enemies and redeeming us from their power. In the twentieth century this conviction is as true to the life of the Church and as essential in its faith as it was in the first. And if we take seriously the idea that this saving act occurred *in our history*, we must think of Jesus, through whom the action occurred, as having fully belonged to it.

Can we go further in demythologizing, so to speak, the biblical stories of Christ's atoning, ransoming, liberating work; in specifying, in a less figurative and more precisely accurate way, the nature of God's saving act in Christ? I believe that we can; and that, when we do, the ground for the necessity of Jesus' manhood even more clearly appears.

Paul is our best guide here, as at so many other points. We have already had occasion to observe the several pictorial and metaphorical ways—surely partly consciously such—in which Paul thought of Christ's work. But his basic conception of what God did in Christ could be expressed in more straightforward fashion: in Christ God had created a new Man, that is, a new Mankind.[1]

[1] The principal biblical passages here are Rom. 5:12–21 and I Cor. 15:20–3, 42–9. But see also Rom. 6:1–11, Col. 3:9 ff., etc. For helpful discussion, see, besides the commentaries *in loco*, K. Barth, *Christ and*

It might almost be said that the three themes—the 'old man', the 'new man', and 'Christ Jesus our Lord' as the way, under God, of the one's becoming the other—constituted the whole content of Paul's preaching; certainly this was the heart of it. The 'old man' was man in Adam, actual 'fallen' man. The 'new man' was eschatological man, man freed from fear and pride, from sin and death, man become himself, reconciled with his Creator, gladly subject to the reign of love, released at last into the fullness of life he was meant to know. Paul was persuaded that in raising Jesus from the dead God had brought this new humanity into being.

And what was the ground of this conviction of his? It was undoubtedly the actual existence of this humanity in the Church. The Church was proleptically and in principle the 'new man'. The Spirit, the very Spirit of Christ, whose presence Paul knew within the community of faith, manifestly had its origin in 'a better country, that is, an heavenly';[1] the love he found there was a divine love, 'passing knowledge'; the peace was beyond 'all under-standing'. God had brought within history what, at its source and in its fullness, belonged only beyond it. In the life of the Church he had given a foretaste, an earnest, of man's destiny—an advance instalment of his inheri-tance. God had set on earth a colony of heaven.

We have called this eschatological, or final, humanity the 'new man'. So Paul calls it. He can also speak of it as a 'new creation'. Actually, however, his idea is not a new mankind *created*, but the old mankind *redeemed*. I said earlier that it is inconceivable that God should freshly create a man—meaning, not only that we cannot

Adam: Man and Humanity in Rom. 5 (Edinburgh: Oliver and Boyd, 1958); C. K. Barrett, *From First Adam to Last* (New York: Charles Scribner's Sons, 1962).

[1] A phrase, perfectly apt, although not from Paul.

think of him as *doing* it, but that we cannot think of him as being able to do it. The fresh creation could not be a man because he would not be a participant in the natural and historical actuality of mankind's existence. Now it is not in the same way inconceivable that God should create, or should have created—on some other planet, not to say in heaven—another kind or order of sentient beings both capable of fellowship with himself and also *perfectly fulfilling that capability*. But these would not be *men*, and their perfect existence would constitute neither means nor assurance of our own 'being made perfect'. Such perfect beings (like the angels of heaven) could be the object of speculative interest on our part, but hardly more. A new creation of this kind would be remote from us and soteriologically irrelevant. The new man, in any really important sense, is the old man rescued and re-newed—*raised from the dead*. Actually, he cannot be the new *man* unless this is true. If Christ, then, is to be thought of as the means of this renewal, the actual 'Way' of this transition, and not merely as the example or manifestation or symbol of the final *goal* of it, his having participated in man's actual existence is as important as the heavenly life he now possesses and imparts.

This is perhaps as good a point as any in this dis-cussion to say something about the christology of Paul Tillich,[1] to whom, with respect to this subject as also to many others, I must acknowledge my great debt. Tillich speaks of a 'new being' as having been manifested in history in 'Jesus as the Christ'. I would understand the new being to correspond, in some degree, with Paul's

[1] *Systematic Theology*, II, 88–180; 'A Reinterpretation of the Doctrine of the Incarnation', *Church Quarterly Review*, CXLVII (1949), 133–48; *The Interpretation of History* (New York: Charles Scribner's Sons, 1936), pp. 242–65.

new creation and new man. But Paul, when he applies these terms to Christ, is clearly speaking of the *risen* Jesus: Jesus *became* the new Man at the resurrection. And Paul's confidence that he did so rests back upon a realized fact, the actual existence of the new humanity—incipient, to be sure, rudimentary and partial, a token only or a foretaste (use any term you will), but unmistakable—in the new community of the Spirit, the new fellowship of faith, the actually existing Church of Christ. Now, as I hinted, at least, when mention was made of Tillich earlier in this chapter, he seems to me to be making implicit reference to this concrete social existence when he uses the phrase 'the picture of Jesus as the Christ', for surely this picture could only have been the Church's picture and could have had no existence till, after the resurrection, the Church had come fully into being. If priority as between Church and picture had to be assigned, one would have to give it to Church. But one cannot assign an absolute priority to either. It will not do to say the Church 'produced' the picture. (How could the Church have become fully the Church without possessing it?) But it is even more clear that the picture did not produce the Church. (Whose picture would it have been in that case?) Actually, Church and picture came into existence together. It was God who produced, or created, both—the Church with its characteristic life and the picture in which the meaning of that life was expressed. But even such a statement gives a certain precedence to Church.

But what, besides certain conditions of history and culture, can be spoken of as historically basic to both?[1]

[1] I say 'historically basic', not 'chronologically prior'. I am sure it is a mistake to think of the Church as coming into existence *after* the event of Jesus' life, death and resurrection. It was coming into being while this event was transpiring; indeed, it is this coming into existence of the

For Paul, as I understand him, the answer would have been a human career, a death, and a resurrection. Tillich's answer to that question is not as clear as one might wish. To be sure, he speaks of 'essential' man as having been manifested in the 'existential' manhood of Jesus. But is he speaking of an actual man, or of a 'picture' in which such a man appears? Does he mean that in the actual man Jesus of Nazareth, essential manhood—or, to use another phrase of Tillich, humanity entirely 'transparent to the Ground of being'—became fully and uniquely existential; and that this actual embodiment in him of pure humanity, of the essential principle or logos of humanity, was the historical cause of both picture and Church? Or, rather, does he mean that this is the content of the picture itself—that what the picture *shows* is essential manhood present in and with the existential manhood of Jesus? It is very easy to understand Tillich to mean only the latter, just as it seems quite clear that he does *not* mean the former. I make this last statement despite occasional sentences in Tillich which may seem at first to indicate the other, more objective, meaning, and despite the eloquent argument of A. T. Mollegen[1] that this is what Tillich intends to say.

Church which gives the event its coherency and its distinctive character. Still, one may cite the career of Jesus and his resurrection as 'basic' in the sense of being centrally creative and determinative within the event of the Church's beginning.

[1] 'Christology and Biblical Criticism in Tillich', in C. W. Kegley and R. W. Bretall, *The Theology of Paul Tillich* (New York: Macmillan, 1952), pp. 230–45. Professor Mollegen emphasizes the following words of Tillich in the article, already cited, in the *Church Quarterly Review*: 'The religious picture of the New Being in Jesus is a result of a new being: it represents the victory over existence which has taken place, and thus created the picture.' But I feel sure Mollegen is mistaken if he thinks that Tillich is meaning to identify the 'new being', of which the 'picture of the New Being in Jesus' was 'the result', with the actual man Jesus. I myself would say that this 'new being' *in so far as it has historical reality*

As a matter of fact, if Tillich meant that essential manhood was actually embodied, or made fully existential, in Jesus of Nazareth, he would be separating Jesus from us and denying the actuality of his manhood. He would be, in principle, a docetist. For a human being as unique as Jesus would then have been could only have *seemed* to be a man. Just because Tillich, as I understand him, is talking of the picture and of how Jesus *appears* in it, and not of Jesus himself, he is not subject to this charge. But although he does not deny, or detract from, the actuality of Jesus' human life, he tends, with the docetists, to define the work of Christ so consistently in purely revelatory terms—as manifestation or picture— as to lay himself open to the charge that he regards that actuality itself as relatively unimportant. The actuality is, to be sure, supremely important, indeed indispensable, *in the picture*; but what about its importance outside the picture? The picture itself is an historical fact of the greatest significance; but what, *of an historically significant kind*, is it a picture *of*?

We are dealing here, I feel, with an unfortunate choice of terms, which distorts to some degree what Tillich wants to say and indeed, I cannot help believing, distorts somewhat his own vision of the truth. 'The picture of Jesus as the Christ' is not an adequate term to designate the reality Tillich sees and speaks of. This reality was a rich, concrete, fully historical reality, from which the picture cannot be separated, but with which it cannot be simply identified. This historical reality, however, was not the man Jesus; it was a *social* thing. It was that concrete sphere of human interaction, that community of

was the Church; and I think this is the necessary implication of Tillich's views (with which, therefore, I am in deep sympathy); but, as I say in the text, I wish he said this more forthrightly and clearly.

mutual response, of which the man Jesus, known as living, dying, and risen from the dead, was the decisively important centre. This, it seems to me, is what Tillich is really speaking of. But 'picture' is not the word for it. The actual communal existence of Jesus with his own was not a picture. It was an objective fact, whose realized meaning the picture represents. It could be argued that Volume III of Tillich's *Systematic Theology* (the volume on the Church and the Spirit) should be Volume II—that an examination of the Church should, according to Tillich's own logic, precede, rather than follow, the attempt to define the meaning of Christ.

So far as the earthly life of Jesus is concerned (and I mean the *actual* life, not a picture, or story, or kerygma[1] in which that life may have a place), one must settle on either the essential manhood or the existential manhood as being the only important, the only soteriologically significant, manhood. One cannot have it both ways; and one cannot avoid having it one way or the other. If we think of Jesus of Nazareth as the Saviour, we must mean one of two things: *either* he was in his own person essential Man (or embodied essential manhood in some absolutely unique way) and became the Saviour by thus manifesting the 'new being' (in which case whether he was actually a man or not is unimportant); *or else* he was an actual or existential man and became the Saviour in virtue of what God did in him—ordaining and ordering

[1] This word 'kerygma' inevitably reminds us of Rudolf Bultmann; and although I am not proposing to discuss his christology, which has points of similarity with Tillich's but more points perhaps of significant difference, may I say at least this much: it seems to me that one can find a close correspondence between the place of the 'picture' in Tillich's christology and the place of the 'kerygma' in Bultmann's (something *shown* or *seen*, in the one; something *spoken* or *heard*, in the other) and that both 'picture' and 'kerygma' are one step removed from the historical reality of the Christ. Further discussion of this point can be found in *The Church and the Reality of Christ*, pp. 18–36.

his career and raising him from the dead, thus creating the 'new man' (in which case the actuality of his manhood and, moreover, its particular concrete identity and character are crucially important). These are the only two possible alternatives. One may believe that Jesus was *not* an actual normal man, a man like us, and that he could be the Saviour only *because* he was not; or one may believe that he *was* an actual normal man—and moreover the particular man he was—and that he could become the Saviour only *because* he was. What one *cannot* do is to acknowledge an actual normal humanity, a humanity like ours, and not find it—in and of itself as the actual centre of the nascent Church and therefore prior to any picture or kerygma—crucially significant and incalculably precious. For Jesus to have become the Saviour it was either indispensable that he be a man, the particular man he was, or indispensable that he be not a man at all. There is no third position. Can there be any doubt that the Church's position, however hesitant and ambiguous she may sometimes be in stating it, is and must be the first of these?

I have ventured to suggest that Tillich, through his emphasis upon the picture, seems unnecessarily—and, I believe, so far as his basic intention goes, falsely—to lay himself open to the charge of reducing the actual human life of Jesus to a relatively unimportant place. Ambiguity at this point tends to be even more characteristic of the so-called neo-orthodox school. I am so far from having read all of Karl Barth that I do not want to speak specifically of him, but I believe this 'reduction' is the effect of some of Emil Brunner's statements in *The Mediator*,[1]

[1] This writer has already been cited as one of the important writers on christology who so speak of the person of Christ as to render inappropriate our calling Jesus a man in any ordinary sense of that word (see p. 38, n. 1). I am now citing him as taking what would appear to be, not

and the same effect can be discerned in other representatives of this school. According to some at least of these dialectical theologians, the action of God in Christ did not take place in an actual human person, Jesus of Nazareth; indeed, they seem to say, it did not take place in time or space at all. It took place in eternity and is only *revealed* in time, and there only to faith. Thus, they appear to separate the essential Christ from Jesus and, in effect, to deny a fully *historical* revelation.

I, too, would say—and indeed have said several times —that one cannot locate the revelation within the individual existence of Jesus (as though there could be such a thing as an individual existence!); one must locate it— where alone, indeed, one knows it—in the communal existence of the Church. But this existence came into being around *him*, and because of *him*; he was its creative centre and largely determined its concrete character. Moreover, the memory of him as an actual human being and the continuing awareness of him as Victorious Spirit are still, and will always be, centrally constitutive of the Church. Without Jesus, and without just *this* Jesus, there would not have been the Church; and without the Church there would not have been picture, kerygma, story, myth, christology, faith, or any other *Christian* thing. The acknowledgement of the historical reality of the Church and of its importance as the bearer of God's healing in Christ—which, recognized or not, is the presupposition of all serious theological discussion among Christians—precludes absolutely, not only any denial of

only a different, but also in some ways a contradictory, position. All I can say in defence of my own apparent inconsistency is that passages in *The Mediator* seem to me to justify both interpretations. I do not know whether Brunner would deny that any logical contradiction is involved in his statements or would simply say that the truth about Christ cannot be stated without logical contradiction.

the actuality of Jesus' career, but also any disparagement of its significance, and, moreover, of its significance as the particular actual human career it was.

It is interesting to observe in this connection how regularly in the New Testament Jesus is referred to as having been 'raised from the dead' (rather than being spoken of as 'delivered from death' or in some similar way), as, for example, in Rom. 1:4: '...designated Son of God...by his resurrection from the dead' (ἐξ ἀναστάσεως νεκρῶν). This expression, with the plural 'dead', is not to be taken as merely a linguistic idiom; it says something distinctive and important. Jesus was raised, not merely from his own death (in some possibly unique or esoteric sense of the word), but from the death which he suffered in common with all other men. He was raised from among the dead, of whom he was one. Here, in the assertion of his human mortality, is the decisive assertion that he was, not simply *like* us in all respects—if that were all, it would not be enough—but that he was *of* us in all respects, bone of our bone, flesh of our flesh, mind of our mind, heart of our heart. He could not now be the 'new man' in any relevant sense—that is, the saving man—if that were not true.

For it is not enough that there should now be, or should always have been, the 'immortal' and the 'incorruptible' (cf. I Cor. 15:53 f.). There must be a way of the corruptible's putting on incorruption and of the mortal's putting on immortality. The once-presence in Christ of the corruptible and the mortal is as essential to his saving work as the now-presence in him of the immortal and the incorruptible. His having belonged in every sense and without qualification of any kind to the 'old man' is essential to his being the head and centre of the 'new man' and also the way of the one to the other, the 'pioneer of our salvation'. It was said in the patristic period, in opposition to Apollinarianism and certain other heresies, that Christ could not have been the redeemer of a humanity he did not fully share. This conviction the Church has never been able to abandon or forsake. But is it not fair to say that we have often shrunk from recognizing its full implications for the normality, and therefore the authenticity, of Jesus' manhood?

For Christ did not redeem our humanity by 'taking' it. We have already been put on guard against supposing that in his case humanity needed to be something special for him to have been able to take it; but it would be equally untrue to suppose that he made it into something special simply by taking it. Actually, as I tried to say in the preceding chapter, a humanity which could be deliberately taken could not be the humanity we know. Jesus became the redeemer of our humanity—or, better, the agent of its redemption—not in virtue of his taking it, but in virtue of what God did in and through the human life, which was not less naturally and inalienably his own for being also, according to 'the definite plan and foreknowledge of God', the creative personal centre of God's supreme revealing and redemptive action.

Our summary, in the first three chapters of this book, of the course of the primitive christology ended with the statement of what I called a poignant dilemma: 'How could Christ have saved us if he was not a human being like ourselves? How could a human being like ourselves have saved us?' These questions could be asked, we are now in position to see, because the original recognition of an act of God in Christ was followed by so intense a preoccupation with the nature of Christ himself as that the original, and only adequate, explanation of the salvation actually found in him was obscured. The more appropriate questions would have been: 'Who could have saved us but God himself? How could even he have saved us except through a human being like ourselves?' These questions, while leaving room for all the wonder of the event and all the mystery of Christ, pose no logical dilemma.

6

PRE-EXISTENCE
IN MYTH AND DOGMA

Up to this point in our discussion of the modern christological problem we have endeavoured to make three
points, all of them concerned with the humanity of Jesus.
The first was that the assertion that Jesus was a human
being has no meaning unless one is saying that he was a
human being in the same sense as other men. In the
second place, it was argued that there is every reason,
from the standpoint both of the historian and of the
participant in the Church's life, to assert that he was in
fact such a human being. The third point was that this
fact, far from causing us embarrassment, should be
recognized as an absolutely essential element in the
Gospel; that, indeed, the Church's whole conception of
the work of Christ—that is, of what was accomplished
in him 'for us men and for our salvation'—collapses if
the normality, and thus the reality, of Jesus' humanity is
denied.

More than once in the course of these chapters, however, and often earlier, we have noted the pressure—what
would appear to be the irresistible pressure—towards
this very denial which belief in Jesus' pre-existence
brings inevitably to bear. We are thus driven to the
point of having to scrutinize, even challenge, this belief,
and to ask both whether we need it and whether we have
a right to it. Before dealing with these questions, however, and in order to put them in proper perspective, we
must return, at least briefly, to a theme touched on at

the beginning of this discussion and consider what is involved in our recognition of the 'story' character of all the traditional—indeed, to some extent of all conceivable—christologies.

This book began with a discussion of what I called 'three ancient christologies'—adoptionism, kenoticism, and docetism—none of which was finally embraced by the Church. The first was left behind as inadequate; the second was surrendered (although never entirely) as untenable; and the third was rejected as false and destructive. All three of these christologies can be recognized as being in some degree mythological—in the first, this character belongs, in any conspicuous or unambiguous way, only to the denouement of the story (Christ's exaltation to God's right hand and his expected return); in the second, to its beginning as well as end; in the third, to the whole of it. To say this is not to pass judgement on the truth of any of these stories, in part or as a whole, but only to indicate something about the kind of story they all are and the kind of truth they may (or may not) have.

I have spoken of three stories; and it is important to recognize that there could not have been more. In view of the richness and variety of the christological terms in which the New Testament abounds, this may seem to be a rash statement. One remembers the many names of Jesus—Messiah, Prophet, Servant, Son of Man, Son of God, Logos, and the like—each of them belonging originally to a different metaphysical or mythological context. The fact that I am not dealing with these names in any systematic way, or with the 'stories' to which they first belonged, does not mean that I am ignoring their importance, but rather that I see them as having only a very limited relevance to the particular issue we are concerned with in this discussion. Obviously, there were many stories in the background of the early Church's attempt to interpret Jesus—indeed, all the stories in which Israel's sense of vocation and her expectations and hopes had found expression. These were all laid under tribute by the nascent community. All the traditional names were appropriated for *Jesus*, and each of them called attention to some important aspect of his significance. But, for all the use it made of them, these previously existing ideologies and mythologies did not determine the basic or comprehensive structure of the Church's christology. Whatever one concludes about the original meaning and subsequent influence of any or all of these earlier traditions, one still confronts the three basic possibilities: adoptionism, kenoticism, docetism. Did the human Jesus (perhaps already the Davidic 'Messiah' or the 'Servant' or possibly the 'Prophet') become at his resurrection the 'Lord and Christ', the 'Son of God in power', whom the Church knew? Or was he to be thought of as having been the Son of God, or the Son of Man, or the Logos, or some other divine hypostasis, *before* he became the actual man the Church remembered? But in that case could he have been, really, an actual man—must he not have continued to be, even in his earthly life and despite appearances to the contrary, that same divine being? These are the three basic questions about the person of Christ, and one cannot ask them without adumbrating the three possible answers.

We have seen that the primitive adoptionism corresponded so closely to the actual experience of the Church as to be hardly more than a simple account of it. Almost by necessity, then, this adoptionism was the original christology. A question may possibly be raised about the inevitability of the next step—namely, the ascribing of a divine pre-existence to Jesus—although, given the whole environment of early Christianity, one does not readily see how it could have been avoided. Once that ascription was made, however, it is clear that only the two possibilities remained—kenoticism and docetism. Either a divine being (called by whatever name), in an act of self-giving incomparably radical and complete, became a human being, one of us in all respects, or else he only appeared to do so. There is no middle space. If we find neither of these alternatives acceptable or possible, and if the original adoptionism is still deemed inadequate, it must be concluded that we cannot state our beliefs about Christ, our understanding of what God has given us in him, in terms of any story of the Christ—if by a 'story of the Christ' we mean (as I am assuming we do) an intelligible and self-consistent narrative of a single personal existence. But if it also agreed that we cannot describe God's act in Christ except in terms of such a story, how impossible the position in which we seem to be left!

Now I should say that this impasse comes about because we do not recognize clearly enough that a story is a *story* and that its truth is its own kind of truth. One must not expect a story of a deed of God—a story bound to be in some degree mythological—to be true in the same way narratives of actual incidents may be true, not to speak of scientific or metaphysical propositions. Am I oversimplifying the situation in a hopelessly naïve and utterly irresponsible way when I suggest that, in no small part, the contradictions and obscurities which have plagued the Church's effort to state its christological belief have arisen from a failure to make this distinction? We have often insisted on taking myths as dogmas—thus distorting the one and confusing the other. May I try to show that this is true, or at any rate why I think it is, by taking as an example what I should say is undoubtedly the most appropriate, and therefore the 'truest', of the three possible christological stories—namely, what I have been calling kenoticism?

Here is a way of telling the story of Christ which *as story* is superb, indeed perfect. Earlier, I ventured to say, and sought to demonstrate, that if, under different conditions, the original adoptionist pattern had proved to be the final one, the Church would not have found it hopelessly inadequate. 'In Christ God was reconciling the world to himself' is really the whole of the Gospel, and that message could have been fully proclaimed within the limits of the primitive story. But conditions *did* become different. The story of what God did in Christ became, by a kind of necessity both psychological and cultural, the story of Christ himself. And once that happened—or in the measure in which it happened—the old pattern would no longer do. It was no longer enough to recognize that Jesus' human life and death belonged to God's saving deed. That deed was now thought of, more and more, as Jesus' own deed; and his entire life, from conception and birth to death, as his own conscious, intentional doing of it. But since obviously he himself must have been antecedent to his own action, his pre-existence was necessarily affirmed; and at once the kenotic story was in being. If the whole meaning of what God did in Christ, as experienced in the community in which Jesus was remembered and still known, was to be expressed in a story of the single continuous career of Jesus Christ himself, this development was inevitable.

I have said that, given this condition, here was the perfect story. A divine being, God's own Son, most high in the glory of God the Father, surrenders not only his status but his very being as divine (one might soon say, 'as God') in order to become a man and to stand with his brothers against man's demonic enemies, sin and death, who held him in grievous bondage. As a man he suffers the ultimate in deprivation, pain and shame. But instead of succumbing to his foes, he conquers them and sets man free. Here are expressed the heights and depths of the divine *agape*, the full meaning of the Incarnation, the wonder of the event, the reality of a new health and a new hope—in a word, the content, the inner substance, of the Church's life. It is, I say again, the perfect story; and in the prayers and hymns of the Church it is allowed to be the story it is.

But the Christian not only sings and prays; he also thinks. And this story cannot be subjected to the kind of critical reflection we ordinarily bring to bear on state-ments of fact and still seem true. As we have noted many times, it is simply incredible that a divine person should have become a fully and normally human person—that is, if he was also to continue to be, in his essential identity, the same person. And without the assumption of this continuity and identity, the story falls apart and the pre-existence of Jesus is in effect denied. Under these conditions, three courses are open: either one rejects the story as false; or, recognizing the nature of the story as story and acknowledging its truth as such, one seeks to interpret its intention and meaning, as best one can, in empirical and rational terms; or one changes the story in the hope of making it more credible. The first of these alternatives was out of the question for the early Church; the second was hardly possible for it; only the third was really open and available.

We have seen that as early as Paul and the writer to

the Hebrews, modifications of the kenotic picture were being introduced and that by the time we reach the Fourth Gospel, not to mention the early Fathers, the sharp corners of the more primitive structures have become smooth and rounded; the bold contrasts have all but disappeared; and kenoticism has been so rationalized, or infused with thought, as to have ceased to be the story it was—without, however, being allowed to become the only coherent story it could otherwise be (namely, docetism). The result is a christology, half story and half dogma, a compound of mythology and philosophy, of poetry and logic, as difficult to define as to defend.

I should say that this is true of the patristic christology generally (and therefore of the formal christology we have inherited), and that it is true of the more orthodox and the more heretical alike in the patristic period. I do not mean that there were not significant differences among Apollinaris, Nestorius, Eutyches, and other rejected thinkers, and between all of these and the Chalcedonian Fathers; obviously, the differences were there and were important. I do mean that the same basic fault —if it is not too presumptuous for me to call it so—is characteristic of them all: they are all dealing with the 'second' story (kenosis) as though it were a statement of fact. Generally speaking, the more heretical make better sense of it as such, but at the cost of the true and full divinity or of the full and true humanity, or of the unity (all of which the story in its own way unequivocally affirms); the more orthodox, speaking definitively at Chalcedon, affirm all three, but do so—is it fair to say?— by sacrificing, even more than the others, both clarity and consistency. They say in effect: 'We do not see how there could be "one and the same Christ, Son, Lord, Only-begotten,...in two natures, inconfusedly,

77407

unchangeably, indivisibly, inseparably, the distinction of natures being by no means taken away by the union but rather the property of each nature being preserved and concurring in one Person and one subsistence, not parted or divided into two persons; but one and the same Son and Only begotten, God the Word, the Lord Jesus Christ"—we do not see how this could be true, but this is how it is and how it must be.'

We may understand and sympathize with the intention of this statement; we may sincerely feel that, if the gospel of God's deed in Christ had to be expressed as a metaphysical or quasi-metaphysical proposition, this formulation of it was as adequate as any could be; we may be persuaded that if we had been at Chalcedon we should have found ourselves heartily concurring in it. But even so, do we find it, literally, word for word and phrase by phrase, credible or even intelligible? Must we not confess that we do not? Surely, many of us must. The consequence is that innumerable Christians, loyal to the Church and its traditions, find themselves utterly perplexed as to what they are expected to think—being told, as they understand it, that Jesus was ignorant as a man must be but at the same time omniscient as only God is; that he was both limited in power (as he would have to be in order to be human) and also omnipotent; that he was divinely impregnable and serene in goodness but was also tried and tested and tempted as a man must be and only a man can be. Explanations of differences between us and the Fathers in the understanding of certain words (like 'person') may help a bit; but they hardly make things clear. It is still true, as a modern apologist reminds us, that 'the traditional Christology...assumed the possibility of speaking of two natures, each with its proper activities, including will and consciousness, without making talk about unity of person completely un-intelligible'.[1] Many of us find it hard, if not impossible, to make this assumption.

What, then, are we to do with the *kenosis* story? The same three options which were mentioned earlier as theoretically possible for the ancient Church are in the same theoretical way available to us. I now put them in a slightly different order: we may reject the story; we may modify it; we may interpret it.

The first of these alternatives, as a practical option, is, I should say, as much out of the question for us as for the ancients. Not only is it true that the story of the Son of God 'who came to visit us in great humility' is so deeply embedded in our tradition as to be immovable, but it is also true—and much more important—that it expresses in the only available way the Church's sense of the divine 'environment' or 'conditioning' of the event of Christ, of God's own nearness to it, of his intimate involvement in it from its hidden beginnings to its end (which in its fullness is equally hidden from us). This sense of God's purposive presence and action, while, as we have seen, it was not lacking in adoptionism, is much more adequately expressed in the second story. God's unique relation to Jesus—his care for him, his reliance on him, the intimacy which existed between the human Jesus and his Father—all of this, of which the Christian is deeply convinced, is said in this story in a way we cannot imagine its being said otherwise. And how, one may ask, could the Church's particular and distinctive sense of the *love* of God in Christ be expressed

[1] Eugene R. Fairweather, 'The "Kenotic" Christology', in F. W. Beare, *The Epistle to the Philippians* (London: A. and C. Black, 1959), p. 169.

except through this story of his Son leaving the heavenly glory to share, and to heal, our estrangement and our grief? But if there is no returning to the first story (adoptionism), it is even more certain that there must be no escape to the third (docetism). We are left with the kenosis story.

As to the second option—an alteration of the story to make it more 'reasonable' and really credible—I have perhaps said enough to indicate my own conviction that this cannot be done. We have noted the failure of ancient attempts to limit the kenosis so as to have *concurrently* the essential reality of the 'form of God' and the 'form of a slave' in one personal existence. Contemporary attempts of the same kind must also fail. In our own period a number of distinguished theologians, holding firmly and strongly to the belief that Jesus was pre-existent as the Logos, but being most eager to maintain the truth and importance of his manhood, have seized on the word 'kenosis' to explain how this could be.[1] But before their explanation is complete, the kenosis has been so qualified with reservations and exceptions as not to be kenosis at all. The divine being does not fully surrender his divine nature (as, of course, in reality he could not): he gives up some of its attributes, but keeps others; or, according to an alternative explanation, he surrenders the actuality of deity but retains the potentiality of it, thus continuing to possess as a man a latent, one might almost say, a suppressed, divinity.

Critics do not find it hard to point to fatal defects in

[1] One may cite here as important and representative Charles Gore, *Dissertation on Subjects Connected with the Incarnation* (New York: Charles Scribner's Sons, 1895), pp. 71–222; H. R. Mackintosh, *The Doctrine of the Person of Jesus Christ* (Edinburgh: T. and T. Clark, 1912), pp. 468 ff.; and V. Taylor, *The Person of Christ in New Testament Teaching* (London: Macmillan, 1958), pp. 260 ff.

this theology.[1] I should say, however, that whereas one fault—namely, the 'depotentiation of deity' which it involves—may be particularly characteristic of this theology and lay it open to special attack, the equally serious one to which I have pointed—namely, the denial to Jesus of a fully normal humanity—can also be charged against some of its more traditionally orthodox opponents, and often with even greater appropriateness.

I have in mind here chiefly, of course, those who are able to speak of the 'two natures' of Christ—a divine nature and a human nature, both belonging, concurrently and in the same sense of 'nature', to Jesus as an actual person. A brief reference has been made to this word 'person' as used in the classical period. It had a primarily 'ontological' meaning—designating a hypostasis or subsistence—and did not have the largely psychological sense it has for us. But it *does* have this sense for us; and whatever thinking we do is *our* thinking and goes forward in *our* terms. Besides, the problem would remain even if we were able to put ourselves fully in the ancients' place as regards the meaning of this term. For whatever 'one Person'—in, say, the Chalcedonian statement—is taken to mean, how can two 'natures' (each presumably involving consciousness and will) belong to it 'inconfusedly, unchangeably, indivisibly, inseparably'? I cannot pretend to understand how this could be—and I am not thinking now of the *mystery* of it but of the apparent *contradictions* within it—but it must also be said that I cannot pretend to the

---

[1] See F. J. Hall, *The Kenotic Theory* (London: Longmans, Green, 1898); W. Temple, *Christus Veritas* (London: Macmillan, 1949), esp. pp. 141 ff. For an excellent brief refutation see D. M. Baillie, *God Was in Christ*, pp. 94–8. A somewhat more thorough criticism, from a more traditionally orthodox point of view, may be found in E. R. Fairweather, 'The "Kenotic" Christology', pp. 159–74. See also H. M. Relton, *A Study in Christology*, pp. 208 ff.

learning of many who do. Therefore I shall not be bold enough to affirm that the contradictions are really there. I shall not even argue with those who, appealing to the fact of paradox in our actual existence, are able to acknowledge the contradictoriness of these christological statements and yet find them literally true. What I do venture to assert, however, and to assert with great conviction, is this: of no normal human being could such things be truly said.

More sympathy, perhaps, can be felt with those who, still trying (whether they think of what they are doing in this way or not) to make a certain kind of sense of the kenosis story, virtually identify the 'divinity' of the pre-existent One and the 'humanity' of the Incarnate. The divine One in becoming human did not cease to be divine, for he became *authentically* human; and such humanity is itself divinity. One may even go so far as to deny that the divine One *became* human at all: he was always Man, even in his pre-existence, and the Incarnation was only the embodiment in fleshly form of a Manhood which was eternally his. This kind of attempt to solve the basic problem—namely, by reducing to minimal terms the difference between divinity and (true) humanity—has been made in various ways. It is likely to be characteristic of the kenotic theology of which I have spoken: the pre-existent One emptied himself of such attributes of deity as omnipotence and omniscience but retained the more important qualities, and in so doing exemplified not only the very heart of *divinity* but also what *humanity* truly is. As H. R. Mackintosh writes, '...all that is Divine in Christ is human, and all that is human, Divine.'[1]

But this way of thinking is not confined to the kenoti-

[1] *The Doctrine of the Person of Jesus Christ*, p. 214.

cists. Norman Pittenger understands Leonard Hodgson to be saying something not essentially different when the latter speaks of Christ as being truly human whereas the rest of us are in process of becoming such. Dr Hodgson points out that the Church rejected Apollinarianism because it substituted the Logos for the 'human hypostasis' in Jesus. He agrees that Apollinarianism should have been rejected, but locates its fallacy, not in its denial to Jesus of a 'human hypostasis' (which would have been indeed a detraction from his humanity), but rather in its failure to discern that, except in Jesus, there is no such hypostasis. To use Dr Pittenger's words, 'the only *hypostasis* ultimately "human" is the "divine" *hypostasis* of the Word.' Not only is Jesus fully and truly man, Dr Hodgson seems to be saying; he *alone* is fully and truly man. The only genuine humanity is the divine humanity of the Incarnate Lord.[1]

Now I am sure we must acknowledge a measure of truth, as well as great nobility, in such an understanding of what it means to be truly human. But the fact remains that man is not God, that whatever the moral and spiritual quality of his life may potentially be (and in Jesus' case actually was), a man is still a man, subject to limitations of a kind to which, by definition, God is not subject. Man's knowledge and power are the restricted knowledge and power of a man. Even his goodness, however kin to God's it may be, is still the characteristic goodness of a man. Actually, however, it is not the possibilities of our God-created human nature which we usually have in mind when we speak of the humanity of Christ, but rather those limitations and particularities, those marks

[1] W. N. Pittenger, *The Word Incarnate*, pp. 100 f., referring to L. Hodgson, *For Faith and Freedom* (Oxford: Basil Blackwell, 1957), vol. II, esp. pp. 84 ff.

of our finitude, those signs of our involvement in a 'fallen' world, which belong essentially to man's actual existence. One must ignore these if one is simply to identify humanity and divinity, or else must define 'humanity' in a quite unrealistic—must one not say, arbitrary?—way.

As a matter of fact, as I sought to say in the two preceding chapters, there is no way of defining Jesus' humanity as different from ours, whether in its origins, its structure, or its quality, whether in virtue of something added to it or taken from it, whether as regards its actuality or its potentiality—there is no way of distinguishing Jesus' humanity from ours which does not deny the reality of his manhood in every sense which makes the affirmation of it significant. But the idea that Jesus' existence as a man was in some self-conscious way continuous with his earlier existence as a heavenly being— and this is surely what has usually been meant by the 'pre-existence'—this idea *does* distinguish his humanity from ours; and there is no way, however circuitous or ingenious, of escaping that fact or its consequences. If, then, we insist on having a *story* which can also be taken as a statement of fact, kenosis is excluded; we are restricted to adoptionism and docetism. We can have the humanity without the pre-existence and we can have the pre-existence without the humanity. There is absolutely no way of having both.

If neither the rejection nor the modification of kenosis is a possibility for us, nor yet its acceptance as a plain statement of fact, it is clear that we must receive the story as story and then interpret it as best we can, in rational and empirical terms, knowing all the while that we shall not exhaust in our interpretation what the story says and only the story can say, but also knowing that without the effort at interpretation the story will say precisely nothing at all. For a story like this can speak to us of matters beyond our understanding only if it has also spoken *to* our understanding—and, within the limits of our powers, been understood. There are two conditions under which a significant symbol loses (or, perhaps better, is shown to have lost) its vitality and power. One of these is when our hearts no longer need it, when all we want to say or need to say (or to have said to us) can be said without it. The other is when our minds, failing to discern in it the coherency of truth, are forced to reject it. For our hearts cannot finally find true what our minds find false. If they could, we should be hopelessly divided and any firm grasp of reality would be impossible. What we mean by 'the heart' in this connection is not something alien or counter to the mind, but is the mind itself quickened and extended. The wisdom the heart has found, if it be wisdom and not fantasy, is the same wisdom the mind all the while has been feeling after, if haply it might find it. It is a wisdom which, far from by-passing the understanding, enters through the doors of it, fills and stretches the space of it, and only then breaks through and soars above it.

What, then, do we mean *with our understanding* when we speak of the pre-existence of Christ? I believe I gave the answer to that question when I was trying to say why the Church did not find adoptionism adequate. When we join the congregation in confessing the pre-existence, we are asserting, as we are bound by our own existence as Christians to do, that God, the Father Almighty, Maker of the heavens and the earth, was back of, present in, and acting through the whole event of which the human life of Jesus was the centre. We are saying that *God* was in Christ—not in the resurrection only, but in the whole of the human career from conception through death. But just because a human career, any human career, is an integral part of an entire organic cosmic process, we cannot say this about the career of Jesus without implying that God was creating him, *and creating him for his supreme redemptive purpose*, from the beginning of that process—that Jesus was 'appointed' to his high office 'before the foundation of the world'.

If we suppose that such an *understanding* of the pre-existence involves denying, or disregarding, some essential truth expressed in the Church's *confession* of it, then, I venture to say, either we do not truly grasp the intention of the confession or else we do not see the full implications of the understanding. To say of the human Jesus, now exalted and transfigured, the 'first fruits' and the guarantor of humanity's redemption, that he had been in process of being created or begotten (in an organic view of reality this distinction loses much of its importance) since time began, and that in God's 'mind' he existed 'before all worlds'—existed as the particular person he was and for the unique and supremely significant destiny he was to fulfil—to say this, or something like this, is to say all that can be said except in terms of myth or story. We are using terms of the latter kind when we say, 'God came to us in the Person of his Son', or 'God has given us his Only-begotten Son to take our nature upon him', or 'God has sent his Son, our Saviour Jesus Christ, to take upon him our flesh'; and, in speaking so, we are confessing in the only way in which it can be expressed the concrete meaning of Christ in the Church. But when we try to explain this meaning, to set it forth in terms of more precise discourse, we are bound to interpret the pre-existence in some such way as I have been trying to state, or else we fall, consciously or unconsciously, into docetism.

If one is asked what happens, in such an understanding of the pre-existence, to the Church's doctrine of the Trinity, the answer should be clear: 'Nothing at all.' This is not the place for either a description or a defence of that doctrine, except perhaps for saying that in my judgement it answers so closely to the Church's *experience* of God in Christ as to have become an almost inevitable development in its *thought* about him. One may also appropriately point out that any doctrine of Incarnation must presuppose the Trinity—or, at any rate, some complexity (if that can be the word) in God. In no serious theology, ancient or modern, has the Pre-existent Christ been identified with God, simply and absolutely. In the very earliest period, as we have seen, the pre-existing being was pictured as the Son of Man or possibly sometimes as an angelic being of the highest order. Later he was thought of as the Son of God or as the Logos, or Wisdom, or Word of God, all of these phrases denoting a metaphysical relationship of the most important and intimate kind. But never was he identified with God in any simple or exhaustive sense. It must needs be so because God (understood in this unitary way) could not become incarnate and still be God.

But to recognize that there are grounds in the Church's existence for speaking of 'God the Father, God the Son [or Logos], and God the Holy Ghost' as three hypostases, or personal modes of the divine being, and also that it was specifically 'God the Word' who in Christ was made flesh—to recognize all of this is by no means the same thing as identifying Jesus of Nazareth with this pre-existing, and always existing, hypostasis. Just as the reality of God is not exhausted in the Logos, yet is fully present in it, so the reality of the Logos was fully present in the Event of which the human life of Jesus was the centre and therefore pre-eminently in that human life itself, but without being simply identical with Jesus.

Norman Pittenger, whose works on christology have been important to me at many points, has been especially suggestive in this connection. It is characteristic of this writer to emphasize God's *action* in history when speaking of the Incarnation: the important christological question is, 'What was God *doing* in Christ?' But although he finds it true and useful to emphasize the *action* of God and to identify God's presence in Christ in this dynamic way, the action is not conceived of as separable from God's reality. 'God's action' is really 'God himself acting'. If by 'the Logos' is meant (to use Professor Pittenger's illuminating phrase) 'the self-expressive activity of God'—that is, God himself continuously and everywhere acting to create and redeem—then, in the human life of Jesus, as the foreordained centre of the eschatological saving event, we can see the supremely significant focus of this Word in history.

But if we are intending to speak with any precision at all, we cannot simply identify Jesus, for all his importance, with one of the 'persons' of the Trinity. To do so is both to distort this doctrine of God and to discredit the Incarnation. I should say that we must refrain from such an identification, not only in speaking of the earthly life and of any conceivable pre-existence, but in speaking of his present being and status, as well. For in the resurrection his manhood was not abandoned; it was divinely exalted and transfigured. He is still the human being human hands once handled and human hearts remembered and remember still. This continuing humanity is absolutely essential to his 'Lordship'. He can be 'our Lord' in the rich, full, distinctive sense which this term has in the Church's devotion only because we can think of him, not only as having *once* been with us and of us but also as being with us and of us still. If this were not true and if we needed to think of him in his exaltation as being God himself, or one of the 'persons' in God, that belief would be as formidable an obstacle to our acceptance of the full authenticity of his humanity on earth as the doctrine of his pre-existence can be. For if it is impossible to conceive that God could become a man, it is also impossible to conceive of a man's becoming God. But actually no such conception needs to be involved in our confession of the resurrection. He was 'raised to the *right hand* of God'. He was not divested of his humanity, but his humanity itself became a divine, and divinely redeeming, thing. Such an understanding is not in the least incompatible with the acceptance of the full reality and normality of his earthly manhood. This, as we have often seen, cannot be said of the doctrine of his pre-existence.

To quote again, and more at length, from Professor Pittenger: 'It must be clear that in terms of trinitarian theology there can be no pre-existence of the human mind, nature, self, ego of Jesus of Nazareth. The only possible justification of such a theory would be by following Origen in his view that all souls pre-exist and that Jesus' soul was "united with the Word" in that pre-existent state. But this seems to most of us unnecessary if not absurd and impossible. Hence we must reject outright any idea of a pre-existence of *Jesus* and along with this rejection an incredible amount of pious error and confusion. Something *did* pre-exist; it was the Eternal

Word of God who is incarnate in Jesus. Or, in the kind of language which we have been using, the Word, who is universally operative in the natural world, in human history and in the depths of man's life, is focally expressed in our Lord's full and true humanity.'[1]

I have more than once indicated my indebtedness to Professor Pittenger. It is certainly greater than to any other single thinker or writer on christology. With the main thrust of his work—his emphasis on the genuineness of Jesus' humanity and on the dynamic character of his divinity—I hardly need to say again that I find myself in fullest sympathy. As a matter of fact, so fully do I agree with what he says in *The Word Incarnate* and other works on this same theme that I should have difficulty pointing to any matter on which I think in a significantly different way. If pressed, however, I would mention one point of possible difference: I believe I lay more stress than Dr Pittenger on the *social* character of the historical locus of God's action in Christ. He is able to locate the Incarnation somewhat more specifically in Jesus himself than I seem able to do. He can say that the Word was incarnate in Jesus, without the misgiving or the need of further explanation which I should feel if I used these same words. I should always need to say, if I were trying to speak precisely at all, that the Incarnation took place in Jesus-in-the-midst-of-his-own—in other words, in the nascent Church. I feel sure Dr Pittenger would not deny the truth of this kind of statement. But I see its importance and its bearings in what, I believe,

[1] W. N. Pittenger, *The Word Incarnate*, pp. 218–19. The actual phrase, 'the self-expressive activity of God', used above, is found on p. 183, and, either exactly or without significant difference, *passim*. Among the 'other works' of the same writer, referred to as dealing in an important way with christology, may be mentioned *Christ and the Christian Faith* (New York: Round Table Press, 1941) and *Theology and Reality* (New York: Seabury Press, 1955).

is a somewhat different way. Still, the word he uses is always 'focus' rather than 'locus'—and perhaps his insistence on that term goes some distance in resolving even this difference.

At the beginning of chapter 4 the phrase 'the divinity of Christ' was briefly discussed. We saw that just as the Church, if true to itself, could not possibly deny the humanity, since it 'remembers' Jesus, so it could not conceivably deny the divinity, since it knows him as the divine Lord. Actually, however, we do not experience the humanity and divinity of Christ in ways as separate as this language suggests; we are aware of them *together*. This is to be explained, in large part, by the fact, several times noted and emphasized, that the divine Lord is no other than the human Jesus exalted—his *divinity* thus being a transformed, a redeemed and redemptive, *humanity*. But it is true also that the Church senses the presence of divinity *within* the earthly life; and we are now in position to see how this can be. For this divinity consists in the central and integral involvement of Jesus' human life in God's supremely redemptive action and the pervasive presence of God's supremely redemptive action in his human life.

It is this divinity—or divinity in this high sense—which makes Jesus' life different from all others. The uniqueness of the earthly Jesus does not consist in some peculiarity of his nature which would make him more, and therefore less, than man. Nor does it consist in extraordinary moral excellence or extraordinary genius, or even in extraordinary spiritual sensitivity or depth. These qualities can be affirmed—and cannot be affirmed in terms too extravagant—but such characteristics would distinguish him only relatively from others, whereas the distinction of Jesus is absolute. The uniqueness of this man lies in the fact that, in him and in what happened through him and in response to him, the God of heaven and earth, of all nature and history, made himself known, in mighty power and with reconciling and saving effect, in an action unique and supremely significant. Through this man—living, dying, risen—God brought into being a redeemed humanity.

It is this new humanity which alone we immediately know as Christians; and we can call Christ's humanity 'divine'—and mean something concrete and real when we do so—only because we have been made a part of a divine humanity ourselves. For although the 'new Creation' is essentially eschatological and in its fullness heavenly and ultimate, yet as the Church it exists also in history, however brokenly and partially. When we use such terms as 'agape', 'reconciliation', 'atonement', 'the communion of the Holy Spirit', 'the grace of our Lord Jesus Christ', we are referring, at the deepest level, to the concrete actuality of the communal existence into which we have been received. We are trying to express its inner quality. It is the actual experienced reality of this communal existence to which every christological statement ultimately refers and by which its truth or adequacy must be tested.

But this does not mean that when we speak of Jesus as the Christ (or under any other divinely significant name) we are doing no more than explaining, by referring to a past fact and its meaning, how this 'new humanity' came to be; rather, we are speaking of the 'actual, experienced reality' itself. For so central is Jesus, remembered and still known, within the Church's existence, and so fully identified is he with it, that to speak of it in any significant way is to speak also of him, just as to speak of him in any significant way is to speak also of it. He is more than the historical cause or occasion of the Church; he is, and has always been, the decisive, creative Centre of its life. He is our Lord and by that same token the Lord, whether recognized or not, of all mankind and of every man. As such he is one with us; and our own true life is so intimately *with* him that we can speak of it as being *in* him. 'For me', writes Paul, 'to live is Christ!'

But if it is true that we cannot think of ourselves as reconciled and redeemed without thinking of him, it is just as true that we cannot think of him without thinking also of God. We cannot separate our knowledge of him from our knowledge of God. The very word 'God' means for us 'the God and Father of our Lord Jesus Christ'. No wonder Christians found themselves speaking of him as the Mediator or the Great High Priest! Christ one with us, Christ one with God—it is these actual inseparables in the concrete existence of the Church and in the experience of the Christian which we are trying in vain to speak of separately when we make our doctrinal statements about the two natures of Christ.

The story of the Only-begotten Son of God, who divested himself of his divinity and took on himself our fallen humanity in order that he might deliver it from sin and death and set it free to be the glorious thing God created it to be—this story became the way in which the earliest Church tried to explain its own existence. Given all the conditions of history and culture, it is probable that this effort at explanation could have taken no other form. But whether this is true or not, must we not agree that it can have no other form for us? This story of an incredible self-giving brings us, like a sacrament, the concrete reality of God in Christ; and the particular distinctive quality of the Christian existence can be represented and conveyed in no other way. So I, at least, should need to say.

But the reality is more than the story and is the criterion of its truth. We may differ about the story—about what its true form is, about how it should be interpreted, and indeed about whether it is indispensable, or even appropriate. But we shall not differ about the reality it is trying to express. Him whom we remember and love as our Brother, we also love and adore as our Lord. Him whom we have known in the flesh and whom our hands have handled, we now know also as the very reality of God's presence in our midst and in our hearts—judging, cleansing, healing, saving. This we know. It is the actual substance, the realized meaning, of the Church's life and therefore the meaning the story of Christ was created to express. We could not say less than this. More than this we could not want to say.

INDEX

Acts, see Luke-Acts
Adam and Christ, 31, 82
Adoptionism, 5 ff., 12 ff., 19 f.,
36 f., 55 ff., 94 ff.
Altizer, T. J. J., 12
Andrews, E., x
Anthropos, 21
Antiochene christology, 62
Apollinaris, 64, 71, 91, 99, 105

Baillie, D. M., 64 f., 70, 103
Barrett, C. K., 82
Barth, K., 23, 81 f., 88
Bartsch, H. W., 4
Beare, F. W., 23, 101
Bowman, J. W., ix
Bretall, R. W., 85
Brückner, M., x
Brunner, E., 64, 70, 88
Buckwalter, O. R., x
Bultmann, R., 4, 8, 87
Butler, B. C., 25

Chalcedon, 57, 62, 99 f.
Cullmann, O., ix, 23
Cyril of Alexandria, 63 f.

Dibelius, M., 23
Divinity of Christ, viii, 54 ff.,
113 ff.
Docetism, 16 f., 26 ff., 32, 51,
70 f., 79 f., 94 ff., 109
Duncan, G., ix

Ebionites, 62
Eutyches, 70 f., 99
Eutychus, 70
Event as a christological category,
57 ff.

Fairweather, E. R., 101, 103
Farmer, W. R., 25
Ferré, N., 64
Fourth Gospel, 5, 13, 18, 22, 25 ff.,
29, 38 ff., 51, 61 ff., 80, 99

Fuller, R. H., x, 4

Gnosticism, 28 f., 31 f.
Gore, C., 102
Grant, R. M., 28

Hahn, F., ix
Hall, F. J., 103
Hebrews, Epistle to, 4, 13, 18, 22,
34 ff., 80, 99
Hendry, G. S., 65
Héring, J., 23
Hodgson, L., 64, 70, 105
Holy Communion, 55
Hooker, M. D., ix
Humanity, meaning of, 67 ff., 71 f.,
106
Humanity of Christ: A new Testament Problem?, vii f., 1 f. 5 f.;
grounds for affirming fact of,
74 ff.; importance of, 79 ff.; in
Church's Experience, viii, 2 f.,
54 ff., 59; in Fourth Gospel,
25 f., 51, 62 f.; in Hebrews,
40 ff.; in Paul, 24 f., 27 f.;
reasons for, 1, 28 ff., 40 ff.,
49, 51 f., 79 f., 90 f.

Incarnation, The, 65 ff., 89 f., 104,
112 f.
Incarnationism, 14 f., 19 ff., 38

Jeremias, J., ix, 32

Käsemann, E., 32
Kegley, C. W., 85
Kenosis, 12 ff., 16 ff., 37, 43, 94 ff.
Kerygma, 87
Knox, W. L., 21
Kraeling, C. H., 21

Logos (or Word), 21 ff., 29, 36,
60 f., 109 ff.
Lohmeyer, E., 23, 32
Lucifer, 23
Luke-Acts, 5 ff., 9, 19 f.